EARLY EIGHTEENTH CENTURY BRITAIN
1700–39

Lorna Coventry

SHIRE LIVING HISTORIES
How we worked • How we played • How we lived

Published in Great Britain in 2011 by Shire Publications Ltd,
Midland House, West Way, Botley, Oxford OX2 0PH,
United Kingdom.
44-02 23rd Street, Suite 219, Long Island City, NY 11101,
USA.

E-mail: shire@shirebooks.co.uk   www.shirebooks.co.uk

A CIP catalogue record for this book is available from the
British Library.

Shire Living Histories no. 12. ISBN-13: 978 0 74780 837 4

Lorna Coventry has asserted her right under the
Copyright, Designs and Patents Act, 1988, to be identified
as the author of this book.

Designed by Myriam Bell Design, France and typeset in
Perpetua, Jenson Text and Gill Sans.

Printed in China through Worldprint Ltd.

11 12 13 14 15   10 9 8 7 6 5 4 3 2 1

COVER IMAGE
Covent Garden Piazza and Market, later 18th century, John
Collet. (© Museum of London, UK / The Bridgeman Art
Library)

PHOTOGRAPH ACKNOWLEDGEMENTS

Ashmolean Museum, University of Oxford, page 14; The
Bodleian Library, University of Oxford, page 37 (Firth a.3,
fol. 123); The Bridgeman Art Library: Houses of
Parliament, Westminster, London, UK, page 4, National
Portrait Gallery, London, UK, page 6, Private Collection,
pages 10 (bottom), 11, 38, 55 (top), Metropolitan
Museum of Art, New York, USA, page 17 (top), ©
Bonhams, London, UK, page 18 (top), Osterley Park,
Middlesex, UK / The Stapleton Collection, page 26, Roy
Miles Fine Paintings, page 61, Musée de Picardie, Amiens,
France / Giraudon, page 64, Musée de l'Hotel-Dieu,
Beaune, France / Archives Charmet, page 70; Trustees of
the British Museum, pages 8 (top and bottom), 9, 10
(top), 12, 16, 17 (bottom), 19 (top), 20, 25 (top and
bottom), 27, 29 (top and bottom), 32 (left and right), 34,
35, 36 (top), 41 (top and bottom), 42 (top and bottom),
46 (top and bottom), 47 (bottom), 49 (top), 50, 51, 52
(top and bottom), 53 (top and bottom), 54 (bottom), 55
(bottom), 58 (top and bottom), 59 (top and bottom), 60
(top and bottom), 62, 63, 66 (top), 67 (top and bottom),
69 (top and bottom), 72 (bottom), 73 (bottom), 75 (top),
77; Corbis, pages 33 (top and bottom); By Permission of
the Trustees of Dulwich Picture Gallery, pages 44, 56;
Department of Engineering, Oxford University, page 74;
English Heritage Picture Library, page 24; English
Heritage NMR, page 22; Getty Images, page 66 (bottom);
The Museum of London, page 47 (top); St Fagans National
History Museum, page 21; Topfoto / The Print
Collector / HIP, page 30; Topfoto / HIP, page 36 (bottom);
V&A Images / Victoria and Albert Museum, pages 18
(bottom), 48, 49 (bottom), 68; La Ville de Marseille, page
75 (bottom). All other images from the author's
collection.

AUTHOR'S ACKNOWLEDGEMENTS

While there are many people who have helped in the
creation of this book, particular thanks have to go to the
staff of the Kensington and Chelsea Library and the British
Museum for their help, and to my editor Ruth Sheppard
for her patience. Thanks also go to my partner Alex Flach
without whom there would simply be no book.

Shire Publications is supporting the Woodland Trust, the UK's leading woodland conservation charity, by funding the dedication of trees.

CONTENTS

PREFACE 4

INTRODUCTION 6

HOME AND FAMILY 14

NEIGHBOURHOOD AND COMMUNITY 22

WORK 30

FOOD 38

SHOPPING AND STYLE 44

TRANSPORT AND TRAVEL 50

RELAXATION AND ENTERTAINMENT 56

CHILDHOOD AND EDUCATION 64

HEALTH 70

PLACES TO VISIT 78

INDEX 80

PREFACE

ALTHOUGH the first decades of the eighteenth century tend to be overshadowed by the more dramatic Restoration years that preceded them, and the prosperous mid-Georgian age that followed them, they were crucial to the shaping of our modern history. The first decade of the century witnessed the very beginning of modern Britain, the union of the crowns of England and Scotland; and the following decade saw the emergence of the office of prime minister, occupied for two decades by Robert Walpole, the man who is responsible for 10 Downing Street becoming the home of all future holders of that office. Britain's standing as a major European power, too, was established during these years, not least thanks to John Churchill, Duke of Marlborough, whose victories over the French at Ramillies, Malplaquet and Blenheim in the first decade of the century ensured that Britain was never again sidelined in European power politics. The spectacular Blenheim Palace, built at Woodstock in Oxfordshire, designed by John Vanbrugh, was the 'gift of a grateful nation' to Marlborough for his achievements.

War, politics and money-making (or losing – these were the years of the South Sea Bubble, when irresponsible financial speculation resulted in widespread impoverishment) dominated much of the history of the time, yet daily life quietly evolved, prosperity spread and craftsmanship developed new technologies and trades that were harbingers of the Industrial Revolution later in the century.

Focusing on the everyday realities of living and loving, of earning a crust and getting on, Lorna Coventry offers a vivid portrait of life during these years for the middling sort. Her broad canvas ranges from the emergence of organised sports like cricket, to the development of the turnpikes that provided the high-quality roads which knitted together the regions to form a single British economy for the first time.

Peter Furtado
General Editor

Opposite:
The House of Commons, 1710 by Peter Tillemans. William III, Anne and the Hanoverian dynasty all owed their reigns to Britain's propertied elite, represented in parliament.

INTRODUCTION

THE FIRST HALF of the eighteenth century is an often overlooked period of British history, despite the fact that in many ways it marks the beginnings of modern Britain. While history has focused on the dramas of the Tudor dynasty, the turmoil of the Civil War, and the social upheavals of the nineteenth-century Industrial Revolution, the formative era of the eighteenth century has been comparatively neglected. Yet it was at this time that Britain was formed as a nation. The Act of Union of 1707 unified Scotland, Wales and England into the single state of Great Britain. It was also in this period that Britain finally found a lasting solution to the constitutional problems that had haunted it for centuries. The Act of Settlement in 1701 and the resulting arrival of the Hanoverian dynasty on the British throne, at parliament's invitation, established a political compromise between the institutions of the monarchy and parliament in which both accepted the practical necessity of the other's existence. It was parliament's security and effectiveness at raising money that enabled Britain to emerge at this time as one of Europe's major powers, with a highly respected military that it was able to fund and deploy more efficiently than any other European state.

It was also at the beginning of the eighteenth century that Britain saw its first financial revolution, one that formed the foundations of modern-day government and private finances. In particular, it saw the acceptance of a permanent national debt as a staple part of public finance, the circulation of paper money, and the creation of secure investments (such as private bank accounts and government bonds) that yielded stable interest payments. At the same time, Britain's mercantile economy was booming, becoming an increasingly central part of the country's wealth, so that by 1750 the price of land depended on the health of the trade economy, rather than the other way round. Britain's colonies increasingly became not only a source of valuable raw materials but also an important export market, particularly North America.

Opposite: Queen Anne with her son William, c. 1694, by Kneller. William's death in 1700 destabilised the line of succession and the relationship between England and Scotland as the Scottish parliament threatened to choose a different successor to Anne.

The burgeoning industrialisation of Britain's manufacturing sector, such as textiles and metalwork (especially domestic goods) flourished in response to these new markets, marking the first days of the Industrial Revolution. In this atmosphere blossomed the entrepreneurial spirit that would come to characterise the British people in the eyes of the world.

This entrepreneurialism was seen as particularly characteristic of those termed by contemporaries as 'the middling sort'. This term covered a wide variety of people, from wealthy merchants to shopkeepers and prosperous artisans. It would be wrong to conceive of them as 'a middle class'. Certainly they did not think of themselves as having a common identity, but they shared a reliance on their own abilities to generate wealth, a determination to exploit those abilities for the benefit of themselves and their families, and a highly pragmatic attitude to life. While it is difficult to estimate the size of the middling sort by any one criterion, a reasonable level of disposable income is one potential means. By 1750 two-fifths of families had an income of £40 per annum, twice that thought necessary for subsistence, and thus enjoyed sufficient consumer spending power to qualify as the middling sort. The increasing wealth and visibility of the group, combined with the absence of any formal caste system, broadened the British understanding of what it was to be a gentleman, and provided even greater social mobility.

Above: Bank of Scotland banknote, 1723. Banknotes were made out to an individual and until 1725 were written entirely by hand on watermarked paper. The establishment of the Bank of Scotland and Bank of England created greater confidence in banknotes.

Left: Squirrel from Chelsea Porcelain Factory. In the early eighteenth century, more and more people had disposable income to spend on better housing, education and luxuries. Collecting porcelain was popular among women, with items ranging from a modest teapot or a figure like this squirrel.

These economic developments began a shift in the balance of power – away from a traditional landed elite, who owed their wealth and status to their land and had a corresponding set of duties to that land and the people who lived on it – towards a new, moneyed interest, found in towns and cities, who owed their wealth and influence to trade and investment. For those living through the early days of this change, 80 per cent of whom made their livelihood from the land, this seemed to threaten the very heart of British society. These fears exacerbated the long-standing tensions between the political elite participating in executive government, who required the cooperation of the moneyed interest, and the traditional country elites, typified by the bucolic country squire who often sat in the House of Commons. For the first decades of the century, Britain's political climate was vicious and divisive; successive governments were besieged by infighting and vitriolic attacks from their opposition. Their grasp on power was fragile and they were regularly ousted, ignominiously, by political crises, both real and imagined.

The atmosphere of suspicion and hostility was stoked by the very real threat of invasion by the Jacobites, who refused to acknowledge the Hanoverian monarchy, and championed the claim to the throne of James II's son, the 'Old Pretender'. The Jacobites enjoyed the support of France and Spain, and the spectre of their armies invading British soil haunted the political and popular imagination. The Jacobite cause was also supported within the country by those who could not stomach the cynical pragmatism of the political elite in choosing the Electors of

Bath, mid-eighteenth century. Increasing wealth enabled more people to travel for pleasure; visiting family, friends and resorts such as Bath. At the centre of Bath society was a 'Company' of about five hundred selected by Beau Nash, the Master of Ceremonies, from the aristocracy, gentry and the self-made.

Above: *The Turncoats*, 1709–10. This print satirises clergymen whose theology adapted to the political climate. In a tailors' shop clergymen alter their vestments, and one asks if his High Church gown can be altered to Low Church on occasion.

Hanover over numerous, more legitimate Stuart claimants. In 1715 and 1745, this fear was realised with the Jacobite uprisings, while there were further attempted rebellions in 1708, 1719, 1744 and 1759. The culture of fear and distrust this created was felt at every level of society. Those who secretly toasted the Stuart dynasty at their dinner tables ran the very serious risk of being denounced as traitors by their neighbours, and also lived in fear of being uncovered by government spies (who included Daniel Defoe among their ranks).

The political and economic tensions came to a head with the South Sea Bubble crisis of 1720. The South Sea Company had been formed in order to provide an alternative means of servicing the national debt to the Bank of England. It expanded the opportunity for anyone to invest

Right: John Wesley preaching. The cynicism of the clergy disenchanted many and was one catalyst for the Great Awakening: a reignition of personal religious fervour in the 1730s and 1740s. John Wesley and George Whitefield fronted a campaign for reform that eventually evolved into Methodism.

in the national debt, an opportunity that had previously been enjoyed only by major investors, who had profited greatly from it in the previous decades. The opportunity was seized by a wide range of investors, from modestly wealthy widows investing what money they had, to major landowners, some of whom sold off significant portions of land to fund their investment. However, what seemed a foolproof investment turned sour as the company and the government allowed the value of the South Sea shares to escalate beyond any realistic valuation, causing the first financial bubble and the first stock market crash. The crash ruined many of the scheme's investors, and the political fallout threatened to topple the entire political hierarchy that had encouraged the escalating prices

Thomas Newcomen's steam engine, invented in 1712: the first commercial steam engine and originally used to pump water from coalmines and subsequently metal mines. It made mining substantially cheaper, as it replaced a pump system powered by 500 horses, and allowed deeper mines to be exploited as water could now be pumped up 150 feet.

for their own personal gain. Into this situation stepped Robert Walpole, whose adept handling of the crisis diffused the threat of political meltdown and earned him the reputation as 'the great screenmaster' for shielding most of the government participants. Walpole's unrivalled ability to diffuse tension and promote cooperation ushered in a new political era which, though not without its crises, provided the country with low taxation and a level of stability virtually unknown since the days of Charles II.

In addition to these major large-scale upheavals and developments, the everyday lives of many men and women changed in a fundamental way as increasing levels of enclosure changed the way they had worked the land for centuries. The enclosure of common land and communal open fields had begun in the seventeenth century, instigated by the landed elites who, unlike many of their European counterparts, continued to live predominately on their estates and were willing to invest and improve their lands in order to see a better rate of return. This trend continued apace into the eighteenth century, much of it occurring under the radar of parliamentary permission. This process turned the traditional yeomanry, securely connected to the land they worked, into day labourers or tenant farmers. In manufacturing, the early eighteenth century saw the emergence of workshops and small factories where men, women and children worked not as skilled artisans but as wage earners. These piecemeal changes represent the embryonic stages of the industrial and agricultural revolution that was to change the face of Britain and eventually the world. However, while these changes represented a dramatic upheaval in the lives of many people, they were not entirely negative. Enclosure and other improvement created a vibrant agricultural sector that was twice as productive as that of any other European nation. The increasing variety of work available to people as day labourers, without the extensive training required by traditional trades and their guilds, provided more choice in work, and wages meant payment in money and more choice in how people spent the fruits of their labour. This increased agricultural output and variety of work was accompanied by slow population growth, resulting in relatively high wages and low food prices, meaning a better standard of living for most people.

However the increasing standard of living occurred much faster for the elite and middling sort, a discrepancy that became more and more obvious as literacy and communication levels improved throughout society. The low population growth also contained within it human tragedy. In 1700 it is estimated that England's population was 5.2 million, Scotland 1 million and Wales 400,000; this grew steadily until 1727, when three years of successive waves of influenza and smallpox decimated the population, returning it to 5.2 million in both England and Wales, the level it had been at in the first half of the seventeenth century. Subsequent population growth remained slow and by 1750, England and Wales had reached only 5.8 million and Scotland 1.25 million. Meanwhile in Ireland, population levels were largely spared the epidemics of 1727–30 but suffered dramatically in 'The Great Frost' of 1740, which destroyed the essential potato crop that was stored in the ground. The harsh winter was followed by a spring drought, then floods and epidemics of typhus and typhoid and became known as the year of slaughter, causing the deaths of between 310,000 and 480,000 of Ireland's 2.4 million inhabitants; an even higher percentage than that of the Great Famine in the nineteenth century.

These, then, were the major political, economic and social developments of the early eighteenth century. The rest of this book will try to introduce what life was like during the period. Focusing on the lives of ordinary people, it will attempt to give a flavour of daily life during what would turn out to be a crucial period of Britain's history.

Frost Fair on the Thames, 1740. 'The Great Frost' held Europe from December 1739 to September 1741 after a decade of mild winters. In general the eighteenth-century climate was temperate, but it was punctuated by unpredictable and devastating episodes.

HOME AND FAMILY

IN THE FIRST HALF of the eighteenth century a family home was typically inhabited by a married couple and their children. The elderly did not normally live with their grown-up children, nor did young married couples live with their parents. The aim of most people was to be able to form their own 'household' with their spouse, and if a young couple could not afford to rent a house (owning property was rare) then they simply had to wait. As a result, only the very rich and very poor could marry in their teens and early twenties. Skilled tradesmen and artisans normally had to wait until their training was finished in their mid-twenties, while professionals such as lawyers and doctors might have to wait until their early- to mid-thirties. As a result, the average age of marriage for a man was twenty-seven.

While not all people married, it was an estate that nearly all people wanted to enter. Before marriage, without a home of their own, men and women were fundamentally dependent on others as a member of someone else's household. Particularly for men, being a member of someone else's home meant they hadn't reached full adulthood. Even a wealthy young man living in lodgings, or in professional accommodation such as the chambers used by lawyers or the colleges of academics, could not be seen as a truly successful man. Therefore both men and women longed for marriage.

A home, or household as it was most often called, was the kingdom of each little family and only as the sovereign of such a kingdom, responsible for the well-being of his dependents, was a man fulfilling his true role in society. He had authority over his wife and children and as such the right to judge and punish them when they did wrong. This was not permission for men to be tyrants in their homes and society condemned those who were. After all, if the husband was the king of his household, his wife was the queen and as such was due much respect. However, if a husband abused his position and was unresponsive to the pressure of the local community – expressed

Opposite: This family saying grace is typical of the respectable, comfortable and hard-working 'middling sort'. The wooden walls, stone floor, pewterware and earthenware are plain but the cutlery, coffee pot and adults' clothes are touches of luxury. Note that the children stand for the meal while the parents and adult daughter sit. Joseph van Aken c. 1720.

The Unequal Courtship. As a young woman is pushed towards her elderly suitor, the verse below warns 'What can Old Age expect when wed with Youth, But broken Vows and violated Truth, In vain do Parents force, or Wealth invite, Youth claims young smiling Toys and soft delight, All Contracts else dijoyn the Nuptial Bands, And tie to unpaird Hearts and venal Hands.'

as social disapproval or even in the form of public processions, chanting at him in public or personal interventions – it was difficult for a wife to appeal to the authority of the law.

Deciding whom to marry was probably the most important decision made by an ordinary person. How to choose one's spouse was a question that was endlessly debated in eighteenth-century homes, coffee shops, newspapers and periodicals. On one hand it was necessary to be practical about the choice; setting up a home was expensive, and maintaining it required hard work. A lazy or inept husband or wife spelled doom for both, while a hard-working and capable spouse, maybe endowed with a nest egg, was an excellent material basis for the home. As a result, widows were a particularly popular choice as they had already proven their ability to keep a home, often had a small nest egg and, as they were older, were likely to have fewer children in their second marriage.

Marriages arranged by parents were not uncommon, but both the Anglican and non-conformist churches stressed that while introductions could be arranged, marriage should only occur if the couple believed they could love and respect one another. The church and society deplored mercenary marriages as morally repugnant and prone to failure, just as they did marriage for lust. This opinion was particularly strongly held by the emerging middle classes, and they believed that no one should 'expect Happiness when they marry only for Love of Money, Wit or Beauty.' (Mary Astell) The ideal marriage was one where the practical and emotional/moral aspects of marriage were reconciled in a relationship of respect, companionship and love that was financially practical as well. As Mathew Boulten, a successful businessman, said 'Don't marry for money, but marry where money is.'

Having found a husband or wife, the next step was to actually marry. The vast majority of couples were married in their parish church, by their priest, in the presence of their family. Weddings were small with only immediate family and very close friends in attendance, to whom sprigs of rosemary might be given as favours; a symbol of the couple's fidelity to friends and family after they married. The ceremony took place in the morning and was followed by a wedding feast. The bride and groom might have new clothes for the important

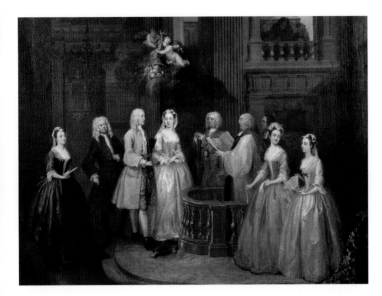

The Wedding of Stephen Beckingham and Mary Cox, by Hogarth, 1729. The bride wears a silver dress and the groom a silver coat and britches with a blue waistcoat. Even this opulent wedding is small, consisting of only the parents of the bride and groom and two bridesmaids, although members of the general public are free to watch from the gallery. The groom was a barrister and the bride the daughter of a barrister. Sadly Mary died only nine years later.

day but they would be worn again. Veils were not part of a bride's outfit and, while a bride might wear any colour, white was not very common as it was both impractical and associated with mourning. Blue was the colour of purity and so most brides had at least a blue hem to their gown. It is from this association that brides today still wear 'something blue' on their wedding day. Only the bride received a ring as part of the wedding ceremony, signifying that husband and wife were now bound together. This was often a posy ring, a posy being a short poem inscribed on the inside or outside of the ring such as 'In thy sight is my delight' or 'Live in Love & feare the Lord.'

Since 1696, the priest had required either the forthcoming wedding to be announced in banns for three Sundays before the event, or for the couple to have a licence to marry from a bishop or archdeacon to whom they would have had to swear there was no impediment to the marriage. However those in a rush or who feared

Posy ring, c. 1710. An eighteenth-century wedding ring, which would have been worn by the bride. These were inscribed with a poem personally chosen by the groom. This one is inscribed with the words 'Content indeed doth gold exceed'.

Marriage in Fleet Street, an illustration of an early-eighteenth-century Fleet Street marriage by Delapoer Downing (1898).The spilled tankards of beer by the cleric's feet indicate his disreputable nature, while the bride's obvious distress illustrates the unhappy nature of this clandestine event.

that their families would object, could marry in Fleet Prison, where a legal loophole meant that the priest could not be fined for marrying a couple without banns or licence. These quick and cheap marriages were so popular that by the 1740s about 12 per cent of all marriages in England were 'Fleet Marriages'; but as they took place in secret they were considered scandalous and condemned by society. At the other end of the spectrum, some marriages occurred without a legal ceremony at all. Known as common-law marriages, some couples were satisfied with a simple exchange of promises and gifts, consummating their relationship and publicly setting up household together with the approval of the local community. However the legal ambiguity of these common-law marriages, scandals where the

Model of an eighteenth-century parlour. Setting up a household required a wide variety of household goods. The bride might bring some with her, but most of the furniture, silverware, glass, pewter and china such as we see here would have been purchased by the groom.

Left: *The Distressed Poet* by Hogarth, 1737. A family lodge in a single attic room, showing how cramped and makeshift quite reasonable lodgings could be. While the poet works, the baby cries in bed and his wife argues with a milkmaid demanding payment.

Below: This modest house has only two rooms on the ground and first floor, and a single attic. It was probably the first home of the Chelsea porcelain factory in the 1740s.

supposed husband subsequently denied the marriage and misuses of Fleet Marriages in cases of bigamy and fraud led to an outcry against the abuse of marriage in the 1740s. It was feared that these marriages, in their rashness and intemperance, were likely to lead to debauchery and adultery and so undermine the character of the nation. Therefore a new marriage act was passed in 1753 that unambiguously made all such marriages unlawful.

Once married a couple set up their home and began their honeymoon, the name given to the first month after marriage when the relationship was at its sweetest. There was no holiday, however, and the work required to maintain or 'keep' one's home began immediately. In an age before effective contraception, children were thought to be an unavoidable as well as a desirable consequence of marriage, but the high mortality rate meant that half of parents didn't live to see their children grown. In the harsh economic conditions of the eighteenth century, many people tried to limit the number of children, but the only effective method available to them was abstinence, hence one of the attractions of marrying a widow was that an older woman would have fewer childbearing years ahead of her.

The Tea Table, c. 1710. This engraving depicts the female environment of the tea table and parlour. The men are outside trying to hear their gossip. An alcove, called a buffet, shows off pieces of porcelain on the left, the collection of which was popular amongst women from the late seventeenth century.

Many households contained extra individuals beyond the parents and children, though these were typically apprentices, servants and lodgers rather than members of an extended family. In large towns lodgers were very common: half of all London households contained at least one. They were a good source of income and their presence did not undermine the status of the family, the key to which was the household's independence, signified by a separate threshold, a separate hearth. The lodgers on the other hand did not have their own threshold and would only have access to the kitchen for certain hours of the day, if at all. Many lodgers lived off what could be heated on the fireplace in their room or bought already cooked food.

An eighteenth-century home was a crowded and busy place. Personal space was a great luxury enjoyed only by the wealthy. Door locks were rare, not only to rooms but also to the front door. Bedrooms were shared; a grown daughter might share a bed with her sisters her whole life. Most people's sense of privacy came from a locked chest or drawer for their treasured belongings, and the private nature of their letters or diaries, which might be written in code.

An early eighteenth-century Welsh kitchen/parlour/bedroom in Kennixton farmhouse at St Fagans National History Museum. A box bed is hidden in the panelling, behind a built-in bench. Pierced panels above the sliding doors provided ventilation so that the doors could be closed when the bed was occupied.

A poor family might live in just one room, which also served as a workroom, while the very poor might rent a space in a shared bed on a nightly basis. For the middling sort, however, accommodation was considerably better. Most occupied an entire house, which gave them the status of being citizens, albeit that the cheaper houses had only one room per floor. Rooms were small by modern standards but as that made them easier to heat this was not felt to be too much of a disadvantage. Parents rarely had to share a bedroom with their children and increasingly even very modest houses had a separate kitchen and parlour, particularly in the south of England. Often this parlour was multi-purpose and also served as a bedroom, with the beds hidden under a table, in a bookcase or a cupboard. While this would cause problems in times of illness, it was otherwise perfectly acceptable and did not detract from the parlour's status in providing a setting for genteel relaxation and entertaining visitors, even in small houses of only two or three rooms. Even in those areas of Britain where one room served as a bedroom and a parlour, the beds were carefully hidden-away box beds.

The type of entertaining that took place in such parlours was typically not the feasts and banquets of the past but the new custom of visiting each other's houses to drink tea. The advantage of this new type of hospitality was that despite the high price of tea, it was relatively cheap and easy in comparison to providing a meal. All it required was a set of chairs, a small table, a tea service and enough time to boil a kettle of water, and yet by personally making the tea for each visitor the hostess was personally serving and looking after each guest.

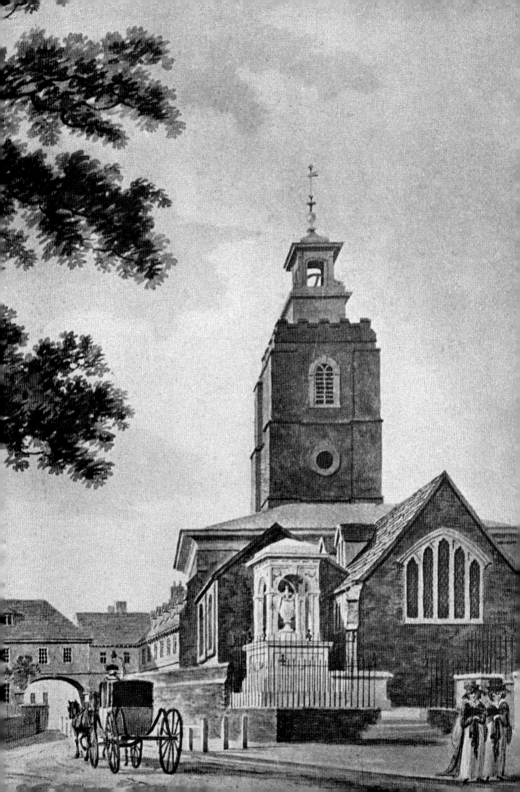

NEIGHBOURHOOD
AND COMMUNITY

L IKE TODAY, people of the early eighteenth century not only belonged to a household but also to the wider community. When people thought of the community they thought primarily of their parish and only afterwards of their country. England was divided into about ten thousand parishes and townships (subdivisions of very large parishes, common in the north of England and in Scotland), each with a church at its heart. The growth of non-conformist churches such as Presbyterians, Congregationalists, Baptists and Quakers meant that not everyone belonged to the congregation of the parish church, but everyone did belong to the parish as a local community and the source of civil authority and support.

The parish was how people defined themselves as a community, and many celebrated this yearly by walking the parish boundaries together, physically marking the line between 'us' of the local community, and 'them' of their neighbours. It was as a parish that people engaged with their collective identity, celebrating national, religious and traditional folk festivals such as Guy Fawkes Night, the birthday of the monarch, May Day, Lammas Day (the harvest festival) and Oak Apple Day, when the restoration of the monarchy was celebrated. On these days special services of thanksgiving were held in the parish church followed by a variety of public celebrations. Guy Fawkes Night saw bonfires topped by effigies of notable Catholic figures, May Day witnessed dancing and processions and the king's and queen's birthdays were celebrated with fireworks. Parishes also celebrated military victories and sometimes the monarchs' birthdays with an illumination. On these occasions fireworks might be arranged, and every building lit up. Most people simply placed candles in each window but some draped their homes or shops with painted sheets or mounted coloured lanterns outside, providing a spectacle that was quite extraordinary in the days before electricity. These community celebrations could

Opposite:
Chelsea Old
Church, 1788.
This drawing
shows Chelsea's
parish church
as it would have
looked in the
early eighteenth
century. The
parish church
was in many ways
the heart of the
community in the
early eighteenth
century.

May Day, c. 1743 by Francis Hayman. On May Day, milkmaids wore their best clothes and danced in the streets for their customers and passers-by. The 'garland' is the pyramid of silver and gilt plates and flagons decorated with flowers that accompanied them.

have a rowdy side as well, one that could easily turn on those who were suspected of anti-socially not wanting to celebrate. Someone who did not celebrate the birthday of the Hanoverian kings might be suspected of being a treasonous Jacobite, while someone who begrudged their candles to celebrate a military victory could wake to find their windows broken and their loyalties questioned.

As well as celebrating together the parish was responsible for the well-being of its members in times of trouble. The parish of Chelsea was made up of about 400 or 500 families at this time. They were collectively responsible for ensuring that no one suffered hunger or was made homeless; that the roads and communal areas such as commons, where they could graze livestock or collect fuel, were maintained; and ensuring the safety of the community. A gathering of the parish or of their elected/appointed officials (called the vestry) carried out these duties and collected local taxes to fund them. Some parishes were dominated by the local landowners or powerful individuals, who reserved the right to appoint the parish officials. Others were like Chelsea which, despite being known as a 'village of palaces' and featuring many wealthy and powerful individuals, had very open parish politics in which all adult men and sometimes women, both rich and poor, voted for the officers of the parish.

The public fireworks display in St James's Park which celebrated the end of the War of Austrian Succession. At a time when the night was lit by candles and torches, these displays were truly spectacular. This one featured fountains, Catherine wheels and six thousand rockets being let off simultaneously.

The way in which a vestry carried out its duties was largely at their and the parish's discretion. For example, they could choose to employ watchmen to patrol at night or not; and while the parish was obliged by act of parliament as well as Christian duty to care for the poor, it was up to them whether to have a workhouse and how generous they would be in the relief they gave to the poor. Therefore the experience of parish relief could vary from generous to incredibly harsh. Even among the relatively prosperous middling families, few could save enough to insure themselves against illness, economic downturn or the death of the husband, and any of these could spell sudden disaster for working families. Extended family and friends might come to the rescue, but equally they might not. Brothers and sisters in particular did not feel an obligation to help one another in times of crisis, especially after their parents had died and the estate divided between the children. Requests for parish aid were, accordingly, common – it is estimated that around one-fifth of families found it necessary to appeal to the parish for help at some point in their lives.

When appealing for aid, families were obliged to claim in their home parish where they had 'settlement'. Today there is widespread distrust of those who move between countries claiming benefits; in the eighteenth century, communities felt similar

A Parish Feast, humbly Inscrib'd to the Church-wardens, Vestrymen, Questmen and Parish Officers, by Sr Guzzledown Tearefowl. This print satirizes the parish officials for their greed in claiming excessive expenses, the only payment they received.

distrust for 'vagrants' who travelled between parishes claiming support and who were suspected of choosing an idle, roving life. In principle, everyone belonged to a parish which was responsible for helping them if they were unable to work, and each parish was determined only to help those who belonged to them and to whom they had a duty. The grounds on which a person had the right to claim a parish's support were renting a house there as their permanent home; by being an apprentice or a servant employed for a year there; if their husband or father was settled in that parish; or for those who were illegitimate if they were born in that parish. For those who did not belong to the parish, treatment could be very unkind, and there are records of 'foreign beggars' being bribed to leave or driven out by force. Some parishes even considered it appropriate to transport pregnant women beyond their parish boundary while in labour, simply to ensure their unborn and impoverished child would not become a burden to them. Women were more vulnerable than men to becoming 'vagrants' and there were as many as three women vagrants for every man, particularly in towns. The death of a husband could quickly throw a woman into poverty if she had small children and so was unable to work. Just under half of women vagrants were unmarried women, many of them servants unable to find work. As a whole women suffered from the limited types of work available to them, none of which required the training and experience that created job security in the early eighteenth century.

The Denunciation by Hogarth, c. 1729. A woman swears before the justice of the peace that she is pregnant by the wealthy nobleman who protests as his wife lambasts him. The accompanying poem reveals that the corrupt justice of the peace will force the nobleman to support her and her child.

For those who were settled in the parish, support could be generous and kindly given. A family of good reputation who, despite hard work, could not make ends meet or who had unluckily fallen on hard times, might have their income supplemented. Surviving documents show that such families' expenses often included relative luxuries such as tea and sugar, in addition to bread and reasonable quantities of meat, as well as large one-off expenses like children's apprenticeships and repairs to their house.

While those settled within a parish were entitled to support, as the century progressed families would increasingly only request support if absolutely necessary. This was because new practices such as making parish pensioners wear a badge and having their belongings publicly inventoried meant that asking the parish for help became far less appealing. The first half of the eighteenth century also saw a boom in the development of workhouses; Chelsea opened its workhouse in 1735. The name 'workhouse' came from the idea that it was good for the parish to provide those unable to find employment with some sort of work, which it was hoped might fund their expenses but in reality almost never did. At the Chelsea workhouse, girls made buttons and women spun yarn. Workhouses were primarily designed for those unable to maintain a household of their own: the sick, the elderly, children and those who didn't have a home, such as unemployed domestic and farm servants. This was not the workhouse of the nineteenth century, designed to humiliate its inmates, but it nevertheless felt that way to many.

In contrast to the workhouse, houses of correction and bridewells were intended to humiliate and imply shame on those sent there. Houses of correction were not prisons in the first half of the eighteenth century.

Prisons were for debtors or those awaiting trial, execution or deportation. In contrast, bridewells and houses of correction were designed to provide a short rehabilitative experience of hard labour for those guilty of idleness and immorality rather than criminal acts. The justices of the peace or magistrates sent individuals there for offences such as having a child out of wedlock, drunkenness, prostitution (which was not explicitly illegal) and petty pilfering. Strangely, they were often also the location of a sort of industrial boarding

In the House of Correction by Hogarth, 1732. Prostitutes and a card-player getting a short, sharp shock in the London bridewell. They are forced to beat hemp for rope-making. At right, a man is in pillory inscribed with the words 'Better to work than stand thus'.

Pillory was a much harsher punishment than the stocks, which only constrained the legs. Pillory was used for more serious offences, such as perjury, and the crowds could be much more violent, sometimes even throwing stones. Unable to dodge objects, this could result in serious injury or even death.

school for poor children of the parish. The residency of offenders was never permanent and it was hoped that once 'corrected', individuals would be able to return to the local community.

The magistrates or justices of the peace who oversaw houses of correction were responsible for maintaining the peace of the local community. They provided law enforcement below the criminal courts and were judge and jury for the minor crimes known as misdemeanours. The primary aim of justices of the peace was social harmony rather than punishment. Close to half of all cases brought before them were conflicts and arguments between neighbours and within families, and the justices' first aim was to promote true peace and reconciliation between the parties. As a result, 75 per cent of cases of personal conflict saw no formal action taken. For very serious cases offenders were subject to 'binding over' – made to swear not to offend again. If they broke their promise they were fined. This procedure was even used in cases of manslaughter, which often was not considered a criminal act, and even when it was, was punishable only by branding on the thumb. As well as personal conflict, the other main areas that justices of the peace dealt with were conflicts between master and servant, abuse of the parish relief for the poor, and theft – most commonly stealing firewood, fruit and vegetables from other people's land. For the last two of these offences formal action was more commonly taken. Those who were found guilty by the justices of the peace were commonly fined, put in the stocks, committed to houses of correction or whipped.

While the justices of the peace, the state's representatives, were generally reluctant to prosecute, private individuals or groups might take it upon themselves to prosecute certain cases. A very prominent example of this was the proliferation of Societies for the Reformation of Manners. These societies began in 1690s London as people rebelled against the excesses of the Restoration. Fighting for respectability, stability and seriousness, they were particularly concerned with policing sexual morality and brought prosecutions against both brothels and molly houses (brothels for homosexuals). They flourished in towns and cities across Britain during the first half of the eighteenth century and individuals found themselves prosecuted and punished with fines and pillory for disrespectable practices such as swearing, drunkenness, gambling, and working on Sundays.

At the other end of the spectrum, serious criminal offences, called felonies, were dealt with in the criminal courts. There punishments were harsh, including branding, deportation and execution. At the beginning of the eighteenth century there were fifty crimes that carried the punishment of execution. The number grew very quickly as the century progressed, and the Waltham Black Act of 1723 added another fifty in one fell swoop. The increasing severity of criminal legislation was not in tune with the feelings of society. Therefore, although more felonies came before the criminal courts, judges actually dispensed the death sentence less often in favour of transportation, branding and even pardons. The severe punishments also made justices of the peace unwilling to charge individuals with felonies and send them to the criminal courts.

Above: Public executions were normally held on public holidays or at least on market days, when large numbers of people could witness the event.

Left: A prostitute being arrested by John Gonson and three bailiffs, as painted by Hogarth in 1732. John Gonson was a justice of the peace and supporter of the Society for the Reformation of Manners. Not all justices or magistrates took the prosecutions brought by the Society as seriously as Gonson did.

WORK

WHILE there was relative prosperity in the first half of the eighteenth century, it was still a world where the vast majority had to work extremely hard to maintain themselves. Only the wealthy minority, the gentry and aristocracy, did not have to work, and even they generally lived busy lives. For every wealthy lady who lay in bed until midday there was an equally wealthy lady who was in her kitchen by six o'clock, managing her staff and household. At the other end of the spectrum the very poor, who survived on allowances and pensions from the parish, might not work; but most of those who received such benefits were either working and had their income topped up or were simply unable to work from illness or infirmity.

Most people began work young: children worked either in the family trade alongside their father or alongside their mother taking care of the home, as well as receiving education at home and/or at school. Such work was not thought to be bad for children; on the contrary, it was thought to be essential training for them to learn to lead an independent and productive life. Boys in their early teens could be apprenticed into the skilled trades, a formal arrangement whereby they paid an indenture to enter the household of a 'master' of their chosen trade where they would receive the training to become journeymen. The name 'journeyman' comes from the French *journée*, meaning day, referring to the fact that a journeyman was paid by the day for his work. Once a journeyman had demonstrated his skills to his guild and saved enough capital to set up his own workshop, he became a master with his own apprentices and journeymen. This formal route of entry into a trade and training provided job security, expertise and even the promise of eventual independence, as most journeymen in the first half of the eighteenth century could be reasonably certain of becoming masters themselves.

Not all families could afford the cost of purchasing an apprenticeship, nor did every apprentice become a journeyman.

Opposite: A brewhouse. From the beginning of the eighteenth century, beer was brewed increasingly in breweries rather than in inns and pubs. While most breweries only employed a handful of people, the scale on which they produced beer was clearly industrial.

Above left: Plate 4 from Hogarth's *Industry and Idleness*, 1747. Hogarth created this series to try to encourage working children to do their best, by illustrating the repercussions of their behaviour. Here the industrious apprentice is managing his master's business.

Above right: Plate 5 from Hogarth's *Industry and Idleness*, 1747. The idle apprentice is either sent to sea by his master or simply thrown out. He is about to start work as a seaman and prepares to cast his indentures into the sea.

On the contrary, the runaway apprentice who had broken his indentures was a common figure. For those without apprenticeships or employment, there were work fairs each Michaelmas on 28 September. This included most women and girls as by the beginning of the eighteenth century, girls rarely entered apprenticeships, even in those trades where they dominated the skilled workforce such as dress- and hat-making. Instead they were trained on a less formal footing, which meant that they were rarely required to pay an indenture but did not receive from their employers the same commitment to train them for seven to nine years.

Other than apprenticeships and work fairs the most important route to employment was personal recommendation. Today the patronage of the eighteenth century looks like nepotism and even corruption. However in a world without job adverts, job agencies, standardised education or examinations, it was often the only method employers had to find and to assess the people they were going to employ. Personal reputation was everything in such a world and there was no divide between people's personal and business lives. Success in trading, manufacturing or finance relied on good relationships just as much as a successful family life or friendships.

Work fairs were particularly used to find employment in the two largest areas of employment: domestic service and agriculture; the latter ranging from farm servants and waged workers to yeomen and tenant farmers. Agricultural and domestic servants were employed by the year from Michaelmas to Michaelmas, and only paid at the end of their year. Poorly paid for long hours that involved a wide range of heavy physical work, domestic servants generally slept in unheated attics or in the kitchen, while agricultural workers were often housed in separate sleeping-houses; simple rooms with cabin beds along the walls and a fireplace to provide warmth. While the conditions of servants could be harsh, the main benefit of these jobs was that servants were part of their employer's household and their employer was responsible for housing and feeding them, and looking after them if they became ill. This provided a degree of security and meant that servants could often save money to invest in their future. Many young female servants saved for a dowry and it was not uncommon for more senior staff such as butlers and housekeepers to subsequently set up inns.

The work done by agricultural servants was the same as that undertaken by yeomen and small tenant farmers and revolved around carefully tending their crops and animals. It was at this time that sudden advances in the cultivation of crops and raising of animals began to revolutionise farming. Enclosing fields, developing specialised market gardens, growing more field crops to feed animals making them bigger, fatter and allowing them to live through the

The Art of Stocking Frame Work Knitting, c. 1740. Husband, wife and daughter work together in their home making stockings. It was a long-standing tradition that unmarried daughters spun as part of their contribution to the family income, hence the term 'spinster'.

Types of plough, 1748. The early eighteenth century was a time of great experimentation and invention in agriculture, as well as other spheres of interest.

winter rather than being slaughtered after an autumn fattening – such techniques supplied an ever-increasing quantity and variety of food to the British nation. However, these techniques needed capital and often more land than yeomen and small tenant farmers possessed. In this environment tenant farmers who had sizeable farms thrived, but the first half of the eighteenth century, which saw a boom in almost every type of work, saw the beginning of the end of the yeomanry and small tenant farmers.

Domestic work, which was mainly undertaken by women both as servants and as wives, was focused on keeping the home clean and warm and its occupants fed, clothed and healthy. This work was essential to the health and happiness of any household and required strength, skill and long hours. Take for example the work involved in cleaning bedding and clothes. The majority of clothes to be washed were white or natural linen, which were soaked at least overnight in lye. Lye was made with ash mixed with water or even urine (known as chamber lye) to form an alkaline substance that bleached the linen. Soap (made by simmering animal fat and lye together and often black in colour from the ashes used to make the lye) would then be used on

Saint Monday. Nine tradesman – a weaver, barber, tailor, blacksmith, cobbler, butcher, carpenter, bricklayer and house-painter – play skittles in a tavern garden, as the wife of the weaver arrives to berate him.

particularly tough stains. The clothes would then be taken to a river or public pump where they would be rubbed on wash boards or beaten with washing bats to work the dirt out. Once rinsed, the clothes would be laid to dry either on grass or over hedges and trees. Fine linens such as headdresses and collars would also be dipped in starch and smoothed as they dried using a slickstone, which resembled a large glass mushroom. Given that this work could take several days, it is not surprising that laundry was only done when necessary and that in towns households often paid for their laundry to be done by an independent washerwoman or laundry. For those who did their own laundry the minimum length of time between washes was generally three weeks and the maximum might be as much as two or three months. In addition to their domestic work and caring for their children, wives from moderately comfortable households often worked alongside their husbands and children, particularly if their father had been engaged in the same trade. This practice began to decline in the middle of the eighteenth century for the middling sort, and a wife in paid employment began to be seen as a sign of financial insufficiency.

While working in someone else's household as a domestic or agricultural servant remained the most common job opportunity, the eighteenth century also saw the emergence of small factories and commercial workshops. For example, the brewing of beer by individual inns and beershops was overtaken by the development of

Chelsea Royal Hospital, with the rotunda to the left. Chelsea Royal Hospital and Greenwich Hospital both embodied the state's recent acceptance that it had a long-term responsibility towards soldiers and sailors, who increasingly saw the military as a professional career. Note that the publisher who created this print reversed the image to avoid breaching copyright.

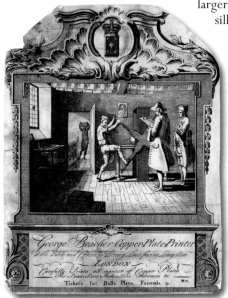

larger breweries. In Derby, John Lombe opened a silk mill in 1722 to manufacture silk stockings that had previously been manufactured by weavers in their own homes; and in Chelsea the first porcelain factory was established in the 1740s.

Working in someone else's household or in a factory for a weekly wage offered some small degree of security, however this sort of work meant relinquishing control of one's own labour and hence independence. Factory workers, as well as journeymen, might assert their independence by keeping 'saint Monday', the practice of taking Monday as well as Sunday off work (a precursor to the weekend), but those working in others' households had no such opportunity.

The same entrepreneurial and independent spirit that led to the creation of early factories also meant that most families ideally preferred to control their own labour and work as subcontractors or small

Above: Trade card of a printer, c. 1740. As the number of journals, newspapers, books and broadsides increased, so did the work of printers. This card shows a customer examining the broadside he has ordered.

Right: Women examining silk-moth eggs and putting them in hatching boxes. This work required nimble and gentle hands and was thought particularly suitable for women.

manufacturers from small workshops in their homes. Weavers were an old established example of this practice and throughout the nation daughters would spin wool for their fathers to weave, hence the name 'spinster' for an unmarried woman. New manufacturing techniques also allowed a greater number of goods to be made by semi-skilled craftsmen in such home-based workshops. For example, Birmingham became a centre for shell and metal buttons, with over a hundred workshops in the early eighteenth century.

For those who lived to see old age there was no such thing as retirement. In the eighteenth century, people worked until they were physically unable to carry on. Even artisans and business-owners who had children in the same trade did not retire and hand over their business to their children. Once unable to work there was the parish and charity to support an infirm old age, but there was no age beyond which men and women did not work. Many guilds provided almshouses for their members' use and the army and navy had Chelsea and Greenwich hospitals respectively for soldiers and sailors who were unable to perform active service.

Woodcut, c. 1700. The working men and women of England celebrate the passing of a bill for the 'Imployment of the Poor, and Incouragement of the Manufactures of this Kingdom' dancing around a bonfire. A variety of trades are depicted on either side with a predominace of those involved in working cloth.

FOOD

IN THE EIGHTEENTH CENTURY it took considerable time, effort and money to feed oneself. One estimate suggests that food represented 80 per cent of a labouring family's expenditure and 60 per cent of the expenditure of more prosperous artisan/middling sort family. For centuries the cooking and preparation of food had taken place in the main room of people's homes, the most important room in the house. During the eighteenth century the kitchens of the moderately well-off underwent quite radical changes. Before, if there was a separate 'kitchen' at all it was an outbuilding or lean-to where food was prepared before being cooked in the main room on a basic hearth, often in the centre of the room to provide as much heat as possible. Smoke escaped through the roof or, if the hearth was in a chimney corner/recess, through large and rather ineffective chimneys. At the beginning of the eighteenth century, houses in the south-east of England began to adopt side-hearths, enclosed fireplaces and grates on which the fire was built to improve airflow. This moved the cooking fire to the side of the room and led to the emergence of the kitchen as a separate room designed purely for the preparation and cooking of food. By the mid-eighteenth century a separate kitchen and parlour was common throughout most of England and Scotland, and a central fire had become the mark of a hovel. Only Yorkshire and northern Wales retained the traditional single parlour/bedroom/kitchen room.

In the cities this change enabled the kitchen to become smaller, making it unsuitable for socialising and increasingly the sole preserve of the women who ran it. In the countryside the change was less drastic; kitchens became better equipped and the average house had a separate parlour for socialising, but the family still tended to spend most of their time indoors in their large kitchens, whether working or relaxing. The advances in the kitchen concerned the fire and the tools used to cook on it; the rest of the kitchen was still very basic.

Opposite:
The Compleat Housewife frontispiece, 1727, showing a new-style kitchen designed to be used only for the preparation of food. This book was aimed at those with a substantial staff, but nonetheless made it clear that the good housewife was hardworking and capable of undertaking every necessary task.

Kitchen, 1760. Although from later in the century, this kitchen is also typical of those found earlier in the century. Unlike that of the kitchen in *The Compleat Housewife*, this one also provides somewhere for the family to sit. The open hearth without a fireplace would have kept it very warm.

No running water or drains meant there was no sink. The houses of the wealthy might have a pump of their own, but at most houses water had to be carried from communal pumps, rivers and springs, which might be some distance away. As water had to be carried in and out of the kitchen, most washing and preparation of food was done outside or in an outhouse.

The developments in cooking techniques were essentially limited to better control of the fire due to the side-hearth and the increasing use of ovens, which might be more easily built alongside the fireplace. The use of ovens was limited primarily to bread: the ovens were small, enclosed chambers made of brick, clay or, from 1700, occasionally iron. They were filled with wood from bushes or small branches that would burn very fiercely, heating the bricks, clay or iron. Then the ashes would be raked out and bread put in. Once the bread was finished, casseroles or pies might then be cooked with the residual heat. The expense of the fuel and the time taken meant that bread was only cooked once a week in those households with an oven; but many did not bother, particularly in towns where bakers provided a cheap and easy supply of bread. In Devon, rural households developed an economical way of cooking bread in the 'Dutch ovens' that had recently appeared on the market. These cast-iron cooking pots were brought to Britain from Holland by Abraham Darby in 1708 and could be used as small ovens set in the ashes of the fire and covered with brushwood and straw. This method spread throughout the West Country and into Wales by the mid-eighteenth century, enabling small rural households to bake their own bread.

Dutch ovens were one of many implements that, due to industrial methods, became available to the mass market. High-quality iron pots, skillets and spits for roasting meats had previously been individually made by blacksmiths, which made them expensive. Now they were made in large workshops or small factories such as that of Abraham Darby in Shropshire, where large volumes of iron implements were cast in individual moulds of baked sand. High-quality cooking instruments thus became available to all but the poorest, giving cooks greater control over their cooking. The most difficult aspect of cooking to control was the temperature of the fire. Wood was burnt in most of the country, with coal or peat being used where wood was not readily available. This delicate aspect of cooking was especially important for the preparation of the nation's favourite meal: meat roasted over the open fire. The meat was impaled on a metal rod which was either rested horizontally on brackets, dangled vertically from the same chains used to suspend cooking pots, or simply held diagonally across the fire with one end in the ashes and the other held by the cook. The cook had to constantly turn the meat on the rod to ensure it cooked evenly and tend the fire to ensure it didn't flare up and singe the meat or die down and leave the meat uncooked.

Fragment from Hogarth's *Noon*, c. 1738. Here a young woman and a boy are carrying home pies for dinner that would have been baked in the baker's oven once it was no longer hot enough for bread. This practice was very common in towns where fewer people had ovens. The man, woman, girl and boy in this fragment represent the English working classes embracing their natural impulses.

Britain was famous for its roasted meats. The French nickname for the British, 'les rosbifs', arose at this time from their admiration of the dish, and French chefs came to England to learn how to roast meats. (The name's pejorative associations arose in the nineteenth

Left: An unused sketch from Hogarth's *Industry and Idleness*. An apprentice stealing from his mother's cook-shop. In large cities ready to eat food from street vendors or cookshops was big business.

The Hungry Clown. A man burns himself with his hasty pudding as his wife laughs. Hasty pudding was a porridge-like substance made with flour and water. Along with the bread, cheese and beer on the table it was a food staple for the less well-off, particularly in the country.

century.) The Sublime Society of Beef Steaks was established in 1735 to patriotically celebrate 'beef and liberty', but the roast dinner was quite different from the national institution of today. Bread rather than potatoes was eaten alongside meat, as potatoes were not yet part of the national diet. Where potatoes were consumed, such as in Lancashire, they were only ever boiled. Vegetables had become fashionable amongst the elites and Chelsea was famous for supplying exotic London tastes from its market gardens; but they were not part of a roast dinner, and were either fine dishes on the tables of the rich, or garden-grown necessities for the poor. Yorkshire pudding (known as dripping pudding until 1747) was part of a roast dinner: the batter was placed in a pan underneath the roasting meat and shaken as the fat dripped off the meat to produce a very rich and much flatter dish to that eaten today. Plum pudding, the ancestor of the modern Christmas pudding, was actually a more common accompaniment to roast beef.

Roasts were special meals for most families: on a normal weekday a family's hot meal was generally boiled in a cooking pot which hung over the fire, as this required far less attention and fuel than roasting. The cost of fuel in preparing a hot meal meant that only one meal of the day was freshly cooked. Breakfast and supper were light meals of bread, cheese, and maybe cold

Maid carrying a tea tray, 1744. The first tea sets were based on the Chinese services merchants had seen when purchasing the tea, therefore the cups have no handles. However, the spherical teapot with a small spout was mistakenly based on Chinese wine pots.

meats served with beer or tea, which required no cooking. For those living in towns, prepared food bought on the street formed a substantial part of many normal people's diets, as did more substantial meals eaten in inns and coffee houses.

The majority of people did however enjoy one substantial cooked meal each day called dinner, which for all but the very wealthy was served in the middle of the day. This meant that people who worked outside the home returned for the midday meal and then went back to work. It was common for the main meal to begin with pottage, a thick soup verging on a stew in which vegetables and meat would be cooked together. Alongside this would be served a pie or a joint of meat, sometimes both. Beef was the most popular meat, followed by chicken; but pork was the most commonly eaten, particularly pickled pork which was gently simmered. Duck and goose were viewed with suspicion because they ate slugs and snails. Puddings were mixtures of bread or grains with meat and/or fruit boiled either in animal insides (like sausages or haggis) or in a muslin cloth and like dumplings could be savory or sweet. If the family was wealthy this would be followed by another course, which would also include meat but alongside which would be served sweet puddings, dumplings, custards and jellies. Most family meals, however, were only of one course.

The most common type of pottage was peas pottage in which peas were gently cooked for several hours, often with a piece of bacon and which formed a solid patty that could be cut up cold for other meals. Peas were a very widely used food on every rung of the social ladder, from the king to the poorest peasant, although the poor had little variety in their diet and mainly lived off pottage, cheese and bread. While starvation was rare, hunger was common. For those above the very poorest, however, the first half of the eighteenth century was a time of low food costs, steady wages and an increasing variety of both types of food and how they were prepared. The drop in food prices was the result of the ongoing agricultural revolution that saw productivity drastically increase. Grains – oat, wheat and barley from which bread was made – actually dropped in price. The dairy industry was coming to the culmination of two centuries of advancement, leading to a boom in cheese-making. The staples of life were cheaper than they had been in living memory, and visitors from abroad were amazed at how much the English – of all classes – ate in comparison to the rest of Europe.

Above: English chocolate pot, 1723. Chocolate and coffee pots were based on tankards, with an added spout and lid and the addition of a small extra lid on top of chocolate pots for a stirrer. The innovation of drinking chocolate with milk was that of Chelsea doctor Sir Hans Sloane.

Shopping and Style

IMPROVED METHODS of manufacturing lowered the cost of almost all goods in the first half of the eighteenth century, opening up a world of consumerism to everyday people in a way that had not previously existed. Towns, particularly ports, became hubs of retail and for the first time people would routinely travel from the surrounding countryside to purchase goods and services. In this world of growing consumption, not only had the established, traditional goods become cheaper but new products were introduced; some imported, like the cottons and muslins arriving from India, some domestic, like the new iron cooking pots manufactured in Coalbrookdale, Shropshire. Everyday people could now purchase items purely for their own amusement. Toyshops began to appear, a toy being any object designed purely for entertainment, often whimsical miniature versions of household items.

In the seventeenth century, shops had played a relatively limited part in the everyday lives of most people. Goods had been purchased from street traders, markets or relatively small local shops. Over the course of this period this experience changed dramatically. With the boom in the range of goods available and the buying power of many consumers, shops took on a far more significant role. While shopping at the butcher and baker was relatively unchanged from the seventeenth century, special occasional purchases such as books, pottery, porcelain and furniture now took place in far larger and more profitable shops and warehouses, as did the purchasing of increasingly exotic foodstuffs such as spices, tea, coffee and sugar, all of which became staple parts of the British diet. The person of the shopkeeper and the institution of the shop became far more important to the financial lives of most individuals and families, particularly as the established practice of shopkeepers offering credit to their customers now became an essential part of household finance. Effectively keeping house now became in part a matter of maintaining good accounts and keeping track of the many lines of credit extended at any one time. This widespread credit

Opposite: *Couple in a landscape* by Gainsborough, 1750s. For wealthy married women, loose clothing was popular throughout the first half of the eighteenth century. The silhouette did change around the mid-century with the introduction of paniers; baskets tied on either side to widen the skirt.

Trade card of George Willdey, scientific instrument maker, at the Great Toy Shop, early eighteenth century. Examples of toys include a telescope, combs, cutlery, chatelaine, magnifying glass and a perpetual calendar.

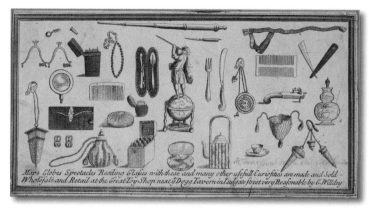

Maps Globes Spectacles Reading Glasses with these and many other usefull Curiosities are made and Sold Wholesale and Retail at the Great Toy Shop next ye Dogg Tavern in Ludgate street very Reasonable by G. Willdey

Portrait of Julines Beckford returning from a masquerade. The distinctiveness of clothes in the early eighteenth century meant that those who attended masquerades not only needed to hide their faces with a mask but also their clothes with a large cloak, called a domino, seen on the table.

system could easily tip over into debt and the fear of bankruptcy, either for the overstretched consumer or the out-of-pocket shopkeeper.

One of the biggest single expense in any household was the purchase of clothes. In the days before mass manufacturing and standardised designs, the main articles of clothing were all handmade to the specifics of their wearer. The design of clothing was very individualised, with far less conformity and no firm rules as to what was appropriate to be worn on particular occasions, or by particular people. The diversity of style, coupled with the fact that the overwhelming majority of adults would own only one or two sets of clothing at any time, made clothes instantly identifiable with their owners, and vice versa. This could have peculiar consequences, such as maids who had inherited their mistresses' cast-offs being mistaken for their mistress, to the embarrassment of all, while thieves who chanced their luck on stealing clothes risked being given away by items easily identified with their victims.

Whether you were rich or poor, purchasing clothes was a significant investment, representing a substantial proportion of your income. People of all levels in society spent as much as they could afford on their clothes. The differences in dress of people at different levels of the social ladder were chiefly in the quality and value of the materials from which their clothes were made. The wealthiest would wear richly brocaded silks that were almost works of art in their own right, and garnish their clothes with diamond buttons and gold embroidery. Those who could not afford such extravagance would use the finest materials they

Although this illustration of a tailor's shop dates from the second half of the eighteenth century, the scene it depicts was also typical of the first half of the century. Apprentices and journeymen work together, sitting 'tailor style' on a workbench.

could afford whether plain silk and lace, wool, linen and ribbons. For the wealthy such extravagance was proof of their status, while for the poor it represented a sound investment – it being widely understood that poorer quality, fast-wearing clothes were ultimately a false economy. Even if you could not afford bespoke clothes, you could afford second-hand clothes originally made for the wealthy from good-quality materials, and since cast off by their owners. There was a thriving trade in second-hand clothes, which were themselves still valuable items and could be adapted and mended for continued use. Buying clothes was thus a form of savings investment, as they could be resold or pawned at a broker for a good rate of return in times of need.

With only one or two outfits in a wardrobe, there was no sense at this time of owning specific clothes for specific occasions or uses – the same outfit had to withstand the physical exertions of the working week, be suitably fine for special occasions, and comfortable enough for relaxing at home. As such the clothes themselves were very adaptable, hard-wearing and generally comfortable. When working, men and women would both wear aprons to protect their clothes. The design of the garments also ensured that they were exposed to the risk of damage as little as possible: men's britches and coats only came down to knee-length, avoiding contact with the ground; the dresses of women who worked were often kept at ankle-length or above to avoid the same problems; while the design of the sleeves of both men's and women's garments were folded back to the elbow or mid-forearm to ensure they stayed clean and undamaged.

Grace Tosier, 1729. Grace Tosier owned a chocolate shop and was married to a brewer. Here we see the clothes of a hardworking woman. Her dress does not have the loose appearance favoured by a wealthier woman with a more relaxed lifestyle.

47

Altering and decorating one's clothes for special occasions, such as weddings, funerals and national holidays, was a significant part of the preparations for such events. One of the most effective ways that an outfit could be embellished would be by attaching fine lace to the necklines and cuffs of linen undergarments. Flowers and knots of ribbons might also be sewn onto the shoulders of clothes or worn in women's hair. These decorations developed into a coded language, particularly used by lovers. For special occasions it was particularly important to be as neat and clean as possible, and the English were in fact renowned for their fixation with cleanliness. The main parts of an outfit could be brushed down; white linen was washed, starched and might also be tinted with laundry blue to make it appear a brighter white. Clothes were generally maintained to a very high standard as a routine part of personal care, while in contrast a ragged hem was interpreted as a sign of slovenliness and dissolution.

Further protection was offered by the linen undergarments that were worn between the main clothes and the body by both genders. Men wore shirts and shorts while women wore long shifts. These prevented the clothes absorbing oils or perspiration from the body and prolonged their lifespan. They were also relatively cheap, and could be bought off the peg, meaning people owned several sets that could be laundered regularly. Both genders wore stockings fastened just below the knee; in men's case they were held there by their britches, while women tied them with garters. Women also wore separate bodices, or corsets, which created a silhouette with a particularly high bosom. Unlike men, women did not wear linen shorts under their dresses. No records survive of how women dealt with the practicalities of menstruation, but it is known that it was far rarer due to poor nutrition, high pregnancy rates, and extended breastfeeding.

The biggest change in the overall design of women's clothes was a move away from the tightly fitting bodices and tall headwear that had marked the end of the seventeenth and first decade of the eighteenth century towards a more natural style. This style originated in the casual robes worn at home by grand ladies, but the loose-fitting dresses gained popularity with women of all classes as general clothing and by the 1730s had become the dominant dress design. This type of design made the quality of the fabric the most prominent feature of women's dresses and helped

English court dress, a 'Mantua' 1740–45. The grandest clothes in Britain were those worn at the royal court. At court, the design trend of emphasising the beauty of the fabric was taken to the extreme, and dresses became very wide and flat to display the fabric to its best advantage. The complicated construction required the expertise of a specialist mantua-maker who would work at her shop, unlike most new women's clothes for which seamstresses were hired to come to the home.

showcase the sumptuous fabrics that were increasingly used. Hairstyles became far less formal, almost negligent in their appearance, held loosely in place by small, simple caps and ribbons.

In contrast, men's fashion did not follow this move towards informality. For men who wore wigs they remained large, heavy and elaborate. Waistcoats, the centrepiece of men's outfits, became ever more ornate. Men wore ever more lace on the cuffs and chest of their shirts, and it became fashionable in the 1730s to wear a waistcoat half open to expose an elaborate and decorative display of lace. Swords continued to be worn by the gentry, in part as a practical form of protection, but also as a status symbol. The most fashionable headwear for men were the many varieties of three-cornered hats. At the beginning of the century these were worn both inside and outside, but the custom died out in the 1720s, after which hats were only worn outdoors.

Children's clothes did not undergo any major change in the early eighteenth century. Their outfits were designed primarily with practicality in mind. While learning to walk, children wore pudding-basin caps, constructed with a padded sausage, or 'pudding', around the crown for protection against knocks and falls. Boys and girls both wore gowns that fastened at the back up to the age of seven, as this made it easier to dress and clean them. The gowns would often have leading-strings, strips of fabric that functioned as reins, attached to the shoulders. Such leading-strings also featured more whimsically in the dresses of teenage girls to emphasise their youth. Young girls also wore stiffened bodices in the mistaken belief that they would protect their backs while growing. At some point between the age of five and seven, boys moved from wearing gowns to britches. However they would not wear formal waistcoats and coats until they reached maturity; instead they wore shirts with smock-coats which could be commonly bought off the peg.

Above: Frontispiece from F. Nivelon's *The Rudiments of Genteel Behaviour*. The ideals of good manners focused on a 'natural' and gentle demeanour without stiffness or formality. For beauty fine white skin, a small mouth and a 'neat' but not thin figure were particularly admired.

Right: English Doll, 1740–50. This doll represents a girl in her early teens. The differences from an adult's dress are that it fastens at the back rather than the front, and leading-strings are attached to her shoulders, emphasising her youth and non-courting status.

O Britain, chosen Port or Trade,
May Luxry neer thy Sons invade;
Whenever neighbring States contend,
Tis thine to be the genral Friend.

What is't, who rules in other Lands?
On Trade alone thy Glory stands.
That Benefit is uncomfin'd.
Diffusing Good among Mankind:

That first gave Lustre to thy Reigns,
And scatter'd Plenty oer thy Plains:
Tis that alone thy Wealth supplies
And draws all Europe's envious Eyes.

Be Commerce then thy sole Design,
Keep that, and all the World is thine.
Gay, Vol. II. Fable VIII. To his Native
Country.

C. Mosley

TRANSPORT AND TRAVEL

Opposite: This print shows Britannia looking towards Lustre, Plenty and Wealth, who stand on the left. A barrel and two packages on the ground and a large ship in the left background show that they have been brought to Britannia by successful trade.

THE ROADS of Britain in 1700 were, for the most part, in worse condition than when the Romans had left. This left large parts of Britain isolated, with poor communication and transport links. Over the next half century this situation was to fundamentally change, and by 1750 most large towns and cities were linked by clean and well-maintained thoroughfares.

The poor state of most roads was a consequence of the way in which road maintenance was managed at the time. Individual parishes were responsible for maintaining the majority of roads that ran through them, and the small size of most parishes meant it was in not in their interests to take more care of their roads than their neighbours. As a result, the roads of stone, dirt and gravel often degenerated into rutted, muddy tracks, covered with the dung of the animals that had passed over them drawing carriages or being driven to market. In wet weather the roads could become flowing streams of mud and manure, making them practically impassable for pedestrians.

It was in response to these terrible conditions that turnpike trusts began to be formed in the late seventeenth century. Turnpike trusts were private organisations that were granted permission by private act of parliament to create toll roads where they collected money from parishes and charged individual road users in return for maintaining them to a high standard. The first trust was formed in 1707, and by 1750, 143 trusts covered 3,400 miles of road, linking large towns and cities, particularly to London. The trusts were at this time very popular. Only present on the main roads, they were avoidable to those who were happy to travel slower, free to pedestrians and cheap for individuals on

Below: A ford, 1735. While the great roads between large towns and cities improved dramatically in the first half of the eighteenth century, most remained very basic, with only footbridges and rudimentary fords.

Above: *Travellers on a Road* by William Byron, early eighteenth century. For the vast majority of people, everyday travel was on foot. Horses, carriages and even carts were far too expensive for most to maintain, and public transport was limited to stagecoaches on the great roads.

Right: Tollhouse, gate and turnpike gate. Road improvements were largely due to turnpike trusts that charged for vehicles and animals to use the road. The name 'turnpike' came from the resemblance of the turnstile section to a defensive spiked barrier called a turnpike.

horseback. Though more expensive to vehicles, they represented such a significant improvement over their predecessors that few resented the extra cost. The quality of the turnpike roads reduced travel times significantly; for example, the journey time from London to Edinburgh dropped from roughly 250 hours in 1700 to 150 in 1750.

The best-maintained roads in the country were not, however, managed by the turnpike trusts; they belonged to the monarch. The most famous of these was the King's Road from Westminster to Kew, which passed through Chelsea. Another was the road (now known as Rotten Row) that ran through Hyde Park and linked St James's Palace to Kensington Palace, established by William III. It was lit by hundreds of oil lamps (the first street lighting in the country), allowing the monarch to travel safely at night. In addition to the king, other large landowners maintained roads over their land which, though used by local residents, were not public highways.

In 1700 the majority of people travelled out of necessity – to look for work or to engage in trade. Britain had a particularly mobile working population, and it was not uncommon for men and women to seek better employment and prospects by packing up their things and walking, or travelling by coach, to pastures new. At the start of the period, travel for pleasure was rare, but it would become increasingly common in the coming decades as more people had the time and money to engage in early tourism. Celia Fiennes is one of the earliest known examples of a tourist who travelled, as a single woman, around Britain on horseback for her health and amusement at the turn of the

century. She kept a memoir of her travels, eventually published in 1888 under the title *Through England on a Side Saddle*.

As roads improved, so the nature of travel changed. Instead of the leisurely and luxurious style that characterised it in the seventeenth century, there developed a desire for speed and efficiency that persists to this day. Horses were bred specifically to draw carriages swiftly, in particular the Cleveland Bay breed. A huge industry of inns and posting houses sprung up, from which travellers could catch public coaches or change their horses when travelling long distances. British inns were noted across Europe for the quality of their accommodation and food, although many travellers would bring their own supplies which the innkeeper would then cook for them.

Improvements to the road infrastructure enabled faster and more pleasant travel, taken advantage of by those with the time, money and inclination to do so. Increasingly, the wealthy made annual trips to London or the spa towns of Bath and Harrogate for their entertainment. The vast majority of people, however, had neither the time, the money, nor the desire to undertake such journeys, and happily spent the majority of their lives travelling only on foot.

A further discouragement to travel was its inherent discomfort and danger. Public coaches were crowded and uncomfortable – with only basic suspension, every jolt of the carriage rattled its occupants. Worse than discomfort was the risk of accidents, which could leave individuals stranded miles from help, or crime, which loomed particularly large in the public imagination. As the wealthy travelled with increasing regularity, the numbers of highwaymen preying upon them also increased. Although the figure of the gentleman highwayman was popularised at this time by famous individuals such as James MacLaine, the majority of highwaymen were vicious and violent robbers, and their victims were often injured and sometimes murdered. The dangers of accident and robbery were both significantly greater at night; enough to mean that only on brightly moonlit nights did people venture onto the highways.

Metal token, 1737, that conferred permission to use the king's private roads. They were given to the country's elites and those who lived along such roads.

A stage coach departing from a country inn for London. Where available, stage coaches provided affordable transport, particularly travel on the roof of the coach or in the even cheaper mud-splattered basket between the rear wheels.

Travelling Etui, 1740. As travel became more common for the well-off, travelling kits such as this gentleman's etui began to appear. This one holds a spoon, toothpick, scissors, and a two-pronged fork and knife which share an interchangeable handle.

Sedan chair, 1732–45. Sedan chairs were very popular for invalids as they could be brought into the house and so transport the occupant warmly to their destination. They became particularly associated with Bath, where many of the streets were too steep for the easy use of carriages.

A major consequence of the improved road network that did affect almost everyone was the increased flow of information it enabled. Britain was a multicultural society, with a variety of distinct local cultures within each of the three countries, and travel between England, Scotland and Wales meant one was truly entering a foreign country. This is particularly apparent when we consider that in Wales 90 per cent of the population spoke Welsh as their first language (in Scotland the proportion of people for whom Gaelic was their primary language was considerably lower, at 25 per cent, due to a successful government programme of cultural assimilation). With better roads the differences between regions decreased as London manners, fashions and news flowed from the capital to almost every corner of the country. Newspapers, broadsides (bulletins) and ballad sheets were distributed by mail coaches along the highways, keeping people in touch with events in the capital and around the world. The impact on the country's culture was profound, as it enabled the development of a national identity, particularly in England. Local cultures and customs remained, but increasingly jostled with metropolitan values, a fact that some lamented but most took advantage of to enjoy a new range of entertainment and sense of inclusiveness.

It was not just information that flowed more freely around the country, but also goods and services. In addition to taking advantage of the improved roads, goods were also transported by water – around coastal routes and along Britain's many rivers. Significant investment occurred during the first half of the eighteenth century in the riparian infrastructure. Locks and weirs raised the water level, allowing barges to carry large quantities of heavy and/or delicate goods safely and cheaply. These works provided an additional 250 miles of navigable rivers between 1700 and 1726 in Britain; an increase of more than a quarter. Many of Britain's most important towns benefited from water transport, for example London and Liverpool, and the engineering works of the eighteenth century enabled yet more cities, such as Sheffield, to enjoy similar benefits, opening them up to the possibilities of the future industrial revolution. The

development of the rivers Aire and Calder in Yorkshire, for example, produced a boom in the wool trade, and enabled the Yorkshire coal mines to be exploited and coal exported around the country.

It was not only domestic trade that grew dramatically at this time. Overseas trade also became an increasingly important part of British life. Exotic goods such as tea, coffee, sugar, and tobacco became staple commodities for all but the poorest families. Britain not only imported goods for its own consumption, but also became a hub for redistributing goods across the whole of Europe, establishing its status as a centre of global trade and commerce. International trade and travel became a fundamental part of Britain's cultural identity. The persona of Britannia identified the country's wealth and prestige with its seafaring and entrepreneurial skill and its trade networks across the world. There was no sense yet of Empire-building. Rather, the state merely wished to encourage merchants and individuals to seek out new resources, markets and wealth.

In addition to trade, some people travelled abroad to expand their horizons and enrich their education. Wealthy young gentlemen began to partake in the 'Grand Tour', in which they travelled around Europe, particularly to France and Italy, to experience the fine arts and culture of those countries – especially architecture, painting, sculpture and fashion. The other notable category of those who pursued their education abroad were doctors and surgeons, some of whom travelled particularly to the Netherlands and Germany where medical training was more sophisticated than that found in Britain.

Above: Dick Turpin, 1705–39. Turpin's exploits were romanticised after his execution in York in 1739, but in reality most highwaymen were desperate criminals.

Below: Coal was transported long distances, requiring considerable organisation. This trade card shows coal being transported from a colliery sea ship into a barge and then into a cart.

Relaxation and Entertainment

WHEN seeking relaxation and entertainment in the eighteenth century, most people would have thought naturally of the company of family, friends or the wider community. The modern concept of time to oneself, or defining oneself by one's recreational activities, was one that barely existed at the time. Instead, communities were the heart of pleasure and entertainment, as they had been for centuries. From the nuclear community of the family to the broad community of the parish, town or country, celebration and relaxation with others formed the basis of entertainment for people from all walks of life.

During the working week there was the opportunity for relaxation at lunchtime (when the main meal of the day was taken and most workers returned to the family home for an hour or two); in the evenings, particularly in the summer; on Sundays; and for the artisan worker Mondays, which might be taken off in the tradition of 'Saint Monday'. These everyday periods of rest would be filled eating with family and friends, attending church, walking, fishing, and playing games such as blind man's buff and board games like chequers. In towns, people would frequent the public parks and gardens which were considered perfected pieces of countryside – St James's Park even had a herd of cows. Families might sing or read together from books of sermons, news from broadsides (early newspapers) or ballad sheets, and even the early novels that were beginning to appear. For adults, particularly men, there was the lure of the public house, or inn, with time spent drinking ale or cider, playing games – particularly skittles – and sharing news with neighbours and from newspapers pinned to the walls. In London and the larger towns there were also the more fashionable coffee houses that were frequented in particular by intellectuals, with individual houses becoming hubs for political and cultural cliques. At the other end of the spectrum were gin houses, where gin could be bought very cheaply, and the extreme drunkenness

Opposite:
A Fishing Party, by Hogarth, 1730–31. This family, relaxing by the lakeside, illustrates the idealised enjoyment of the pastoral that was at the centre of many forms of relaxation and entertainment in the early eighteenth century.

Left: Blind Man's Buff. Games that today are reserved for children were part of adults' amusements as well. Playing rough games or impromptu sports outside, and parlour games indoors, was amusement for adults and children alike.

Ranelagh Gardens and its huge rotunda assembly room were opened in Chelsea in 1741. Famous for its music and its masquerades, for 2s 6d it enabled the 'middling sort' to attend events in the company of the elite nobility and gentry.

that often resulted could have disastrous effects on the health and reputation of their customers.

Punctuating the working year were numerous national holidays that offered the opportunity for whole communities to socialise together. In addition to Christmas, Easter, May Day and Harvest Festival there were Shrove Tuesday, Oak Apple Day and the birthdays of the royal family and military heroes. On these holidays there was generally a church service, which a large part of the community would attend.

Afterwards people might relax at home, but if the weather was fine it was common to gather outside to dance, play music, eat picnic meals and socialise. Most of these occasions were very informal and barely organised but others had, over the centuries, developed into fairs filled with street entertainers and tradesmen selling their wares. A town would usually have one fair a year, held on its patron saint's day, or a day special to the town in another way, such as the anniversary of its founding, or of a famous event in its history.

Above: *The Humours of a Wapping Landlady.* The inn and the pub were a central part of socialising and relaxing for many people. This inn offers music, dancing, food and alcohol at relatively low expense, as enjoyed here by two sailors recently come ashore.

A favourite pastime on national holidays, particularly for young men, was playing or watching sport. By the early eighteenth century, some of the main principles of England's most popular sports were becoming established. Football and cricket existed in forms that would be broadly understood by us today; but there were as yet no standardised rules for any sport, and the experience of playing games was highly local, frequently chaotic and occasionally dangerous. Variants of football had been popular since the Norman era, and continued to flourish in town and country, played on streets and in fields. Games were played between villages, groups of apprentices, amongst schoolboys or any group of friends who took up the sport. The core of the game itself was the same as today – to

Left: Holyday Gambols. This print depicts the popular practice of young men and women assembling on One Tree Hill in Greenwich to dance up it and then tumble down. This was thought quite improper, particularly for women, but nonetheless continued until the nineteenth century.

Trap-ball. One of the many popular bat-and-ball games in the early eighteenth century. A 'trap' shot the ball straight up in front of the batsman who then tried to hit it as far as possible, avoiding the catchers.

move a ball, without use of the hands, to a point or goal. The goal might be a landmark, such as a village church or way-marker on a road, or the game might be played out on a field, with opposite gates

Boxing matches in the early eighteenth century had no referee, no rounds, no gloves, and often no rules other than that hitting below the waist was prohibited and being unable to stand for thirty seconds lost the competitor the match. Boxing was enjoyed as a sport and entertainment by men from all backgrounds.

used for goals – in which we can foresee the first football pitches. Other than these basic elements there was great variety in how the game was played: in some the game appears to be a precursor to rugby, with no forward passes allowed; elsewhere some handling was permitted to bat the ball down to the ground; sometimes the first goal would win the game; elsewhere the game was played for a set period.

Cricket was also very popular. Traditionally played on village greens, it now began to be played in country estates. Although there was great variety in how the game was played, and how a player could be got out, wickets had become a standard feature by this time and the ball was bowled underarm along the ground. Cricket jostled for popularity with a number of other traditional bat-and-ball games, such as base-ball and trap ball, the latter involving a sling trap that threw a ball up in the air which would then be hit as far possible by a batsman.

The eighteenth-century passion for sport and games was heightened by a love of gambling, which of itself was a hugely popular pastime for those who could afford it. Some of the most popular card-games of the time, like faro and basset, could only be played for money, and other games such as whist, backgammon and chequers,

The Gamblers by Benjamin Ferrers. Gambling was very popular at all levels of society, but in groups such as these very wealthy men, fortunes could be made and lost in a single evening.

owed much of their popularity to their association with gambling. In sport, the money that accompanied gambling paved the way for the earliest signs of sporting professionalisation. It was at this time that it became possible to make a livelihood as a sportsman – namely in boxing and horse-racing. Boxers fought one another for prize funds in the bigger contests as well as touring towns and villages challenging locals to try their luck. After retirement, boxers could pursue a comfortable career by teaching boxing and use of a quarterstaff to young gentlemen. People derived entertainment not only from watching men fight, but also from setting animals against each other. Dogfights, bear-baiting and bull-baiting were all common but cock-fighting was the most popular. Cockerels were specifically bred to fight one another by all sections of society, from gentlemen to peasants, and would then fight each other for a prize fund and for the entertainment of spectators who would bet on the outcome.

Outside of sports and gambling, the most popular form of organised entertainment was the theatre. In towns, people from all walks of life attended the theatre to see a range of old and new plays. Shakespeare was already canonised as England's great playwright, but it was the new, highly political plays that drew the most attention. In a period of weak censorship satire flourished, and the government was its main target. Most sensationally, John Gay's *The Beggar's Opera* of 1726 caricatured Sir Robert Walpole, the first minister, as a

The Rival Printers, 1734. The theatre was incredibly popular and was very important to people. Shakespeare was already part of Britain's cultural heritage and this print depicts the intense animosity between printers over the rights to produce editions of Shakespeare. So vicious is the atmosphere that Shakespeare himself is rising out of the ground to try to calm the fray.

highwayman, while lampooning the vices of the ruling class. Political satire also flourished in print, particularly in the journals and pamphlets that grew rapidly in popularity at this time. The most famous writers of the period, Pope, Swift, Defoe and Fielding, all made their name as satirists and pamphleteers, and their search for new satirical forms helped drive the emergence of the novel with works such as *Gulliver's Travels* and *Moll Flanders*. The political instability caused by the warring Whig and Tory parties, played out in the Houses of Parliament, created a vivid public spectacle and the dramatic consequences for everyday life made them a natural topic of interest for all.

The culture of topical, heated engagement with everyday politics at this time was fuelled by the birth of the daily newspaper, traced back to the appearance of *The Daily Courant*, in 1702. The newspapers, along with ballad sheets, pamphlets and journals were read publicly in pubs, inns and coffee houses, often pinned to the walls. They were also part of a great boom in private reading. Weak copyright protection and censorship, and cheap printing costs meant that books were available in far greater numbers, and at lower prices, than ever before. Many of the most popular books were books of instruction, covering anything from learning to read to learning astronomy, and books of sermons or other moral works. The new genre of the novel was also instantly popular, capturing readers' imaginations in an intimate way that was often a profound experience for them. The genre was not entirely reputable however, many would refuse to read, or admit to reading, a novel like Richardson's *Pamela*, thought to be salacious or disingenuous. The Theatrical Licensing Act of 1737, which required the Lord Chamberlain to approve all new plays before they were opened, further encouraged the literary voices of the day to focus their attentions on novels, and helped make it the increasingly dominant literary form as the century progressed.

With increasing quantities of publications, reading became more and more popular. This young woman, demonstrating good and bad posture while reading at home, might have been reading sermons, histories or even novels, although she would not have admitted to the latter.

CHILDHOOD AND EDUCATION

A CHILD in the eighteenth century saw the world, in all its complexity, alongside his or her parents. Children were not relegated to a separate environment or schedule; they ate, played, learned and slept in the company of their family and other adults around them. There was no notion that childhood constituted a distinct stage of life with its own status and quality of experiences – the idea of an 'idyllic childhood' would have seemed as strange to an eighteenth-century ear as an 'idyllic adulthood' does to us.

This is not to suggest that the raising of children was any less of a priority or focus of their parents' lives. On the contrary, in a world where life was so precarious, keeping one's children safe and well, and preparing them for their future lives was a passionate preoccupation for all parents. To our eyes, some of the steps taken by parents to ensure their children's physical and moral well-being can seem very drastic: an urban mother sending her newborn baby away to the countryside for two years to be fed by a wet-nurse; a parent caning their child and taking satisfaction in their tears; these actions might seem to us those of cruel or uncaring parents, but in the eighteenth century such mothers believed they were taking the necessary steps to ensure their child's survival.

In their early years children were kept very close to their parents, generally their mother. Mothers who had to work either worked with their infants alongside them, or, if that was impossible, might send them to a daytime wet-nurse. Boys and girls alike were raised in a female-centred world and there was little difference in their upbringing. Around the age of seven, boys stopped wearing gowns similar to their sisters and in a public ceremony known as 'breaching' would be put into their first pair of trousers. Children were not passive observers of their mother's life. As soon as they were physically capable they were expected to help in domestic tasks, and would receive a steady flow of moral and practical teaching at their parents' side.

Opposite: *Reading Lesson*, 1740. In this wealthy family the little boy learns to read from his mother while she does her housework. It was considered that until the parents' knowledge or ability were exhausted, they were the best people to teach their child.

Above: *The lesson, c. 1710s.* In a far less well-off family it is still the mother who teaches her child to read, on this occasion pausing from her work doing the laundry.

Right: An eighteenth-century classroom. Schools were considered a necessary evil for the children of parents who lacked either the time or the ability to teach them. In this school the children appear happy, but it is still a crowded and distracting environment.

For a child in the eighteenth century, education meant, first and foremost, learning to be virtuous, hard-working and independent. These lessons were learnt from their parents, who might also teach them reading, writing and arithmetic, but the priorities for a good education were primarily moral. Formal education as we understand it today, entailing schools, teachers and lessons, did exist, but was only resorted to when parents were unable to provide their children with a natural, home-centred education, because they lacked either the time or ability to do so.

The preoccupation with a moral education stemmed partially from the fact that in the early eighteenth century people accepted the existence of heaven and hell quite literally. Although there was a wide variety of religious beliefs, the acceptance of judgement after death was universal, therefore those parents who failed to educate their children morally were condemned by society as failing their children in the most serious manner. The moral virtues of hard work, honesty, and integrity were also very practical characteristics required for surviving in the early eighteenth century. Those who were lazy, or lost their good reputation among their peers, would find themselves condemned to a shiftless life; a state which no parent would wish for their child. Nursery rhymes and fairy tales were taught to communicate these values, from the short and simple 'It's a sin to steal a pin', to longer stories, like the tortoise and the hare.

After moral virtues, learning the necessary practical skills to keep oneself fed, warm and healthy were considered the next most important part of a child's education. At a time when a task as simple as lighting a candle required skill and practice with oil, cloth and flint, mastering the whole range of skills needed to keep body together required years of dedicated instruction and practice. It was a parent's duty to ensure their children could gather fuel and light a fire; preserve food; tell the difference between good meat and bad; undertake basic repairs to their clothes, tools and home. A good practical education extended beyond the domestic world, and included the basic skills associated with the parents' employment. It would have been common to see small children working alongside their parents in fields, workshops and early factories – their parents instilling in them the habit of hard work and providing them with practical employment skills. Such a sight would be distressing to us today, but at the time on-the-job learning was seen as a natural part of growing up and the best way of ensuring that children acquired the skills they needed to survive in later life. Thus when Daniel Defoe visited West Riding in Yorkshire, he admired the fact that all children over the age of four were engaged in some sort of work. For children lucky enough to have parents in skilled professions, learning the skills of their trade was even more advantageous. The basic education acquired gave boys a head start if they chose to pursue apprenticeships in those fields, and offered girls the opportunity to play an active role in their family business and some protection against poverty.

Above: *The Prodigal Son Sifted.* Parents took any moral failings of their children extremely seriously. Here, parents sift the sins out of their son, including idleness, tippling, gaming, drunkenness and fathering illegitimate children.

Left: Playing cards which also show the letters of the alphabet and moral axioms. For some the very presence of playing cards in their house was disreputable; for others they were a teaching aid for their children or even themselves.

67

Sampler, 1719. Samplers were a teaching tool for girls in both needlework and reading and writing. This one contains the alphabet and a moral verse.

Given the overwhelming emphasis on parents as the primary educators, for children whose parents had few skills to impart or were absent through illness or death, there was a grave risk that they would be destined for lifelong poverty. It was in response to this injustice that charity schools blossomed in the first half of the eighteenth century, led by the Society for the Promotion of Christian Knowledge, founded in 1699. Charity schools sought to provide literacy, knowledge of scripture, and a positive work ethic that would enable children to enter apprenticeships and trades, and have a productive and successful life. The idea that schools could step in to substitute for the natural role of the parent was very controversial. It was feared that such schools would indoctrinate their children with the religious views of their founders, and that they would educate children beyond their station, ultimately making them unhappy. As a result, some schools felt pressured to restrict their curriculum (excluding basic writing and numeracy beyond counting), and limit attendance to alternate days – sending children out to work in fields, factories and workshops on their off-days.

For children of the middling sort, formal education had traditionally been found in grammar schools, where those who could not afford private tutors were offered the opportunity to receive a classical education. Since Tudor times these schools had provided a specialist education in Latin, occasionally Greek, and the literature and history of the ancient world. This academic education fell out of favour in the early eighteenth century, when most parents sought a more practical and entrepreneurial curriculum and instead of Latin wished their children to learn shorthand, accounting, basic science and modern languages. Some grammar schools adapted to this new trend and provided the desired lessons. Private schools were also founded by enterprising individuals to provide a cheap, practical education to meet this demand. Other grammar schools responded by becoming more self-consciously elitist, excluding the middling sort and presenting themselves as the natural habitat of young gentlemen. They evolved into the famous English public boarding schools, such as Harrow, Winchester, Eton and Westminster. These schools provided a thorough classical education from teachers with a scholarly background; an education still considered a prerequisite for those wishing to associate with the nobility.

There was no formal school-leaving age at this time; most children who attended school only did so for three or four years, and left when their families considered their formal education complete. On leaving grammar school, most children would go straight into employment, seeking a patron or apprenticeship in their chosen profession. Some would go on to further study, either at one of the four British universities (Oxford, Cambridge, Edinburgh and St Andrews), one of the inns of court in London, or abroad. Many of those pursuing further studies would do so with a particular profession in mind, typically the law, the church, or medicine.

The universities, charity and grammar schools shared one overriding characteristic – they were intimately associated with the Anglican church and attendance was restricted to Anglican families. For the children of non-conformists, dissenting academies, such as Kibworth, Kendall and Warrington, were established and taught children from early teenage years through to 18 and 19. They provided a classical education with a strong theological emphasis, focusing on argument (rhetoric), logical reasoning and public debate.

For people from all walks of life education did not end with their childhood. A culture of lifelong learning and seeking of knowledge was widespread, and served by self-help books, public lectures and a general discourse in society about science, philosophy and theology. This adult learning, in conjunction with the better education of children, saw literacy rates in Britain increase sharply in the eighteenth century, especially in Scotland and Wales where the importance of being able to read scripture was felt very strongly. This resulted in a literacy rate of 40 per cent in England, 45 per cent in Scotland and just over 50 per cent in Wales; the highest in the western world at this time.

The emerging public schools could be rough and riotous. In 1716 the publisher Edmund Curll offended the Westminster schoolboys, so they tossed him in a blanket, flogged him, and made him beg for forgiveness on his knees.

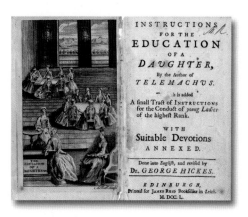

Right: Instructions for the education of a daughter. In the 1730s and 40s the idea of a specialised education for genteel girls developed quite suddenly. Here, girls are shown reading newspapers and books together, and listening to a clergyman.

HEALTH

IN THE early eighteenth century, preserving good health could mean the difference between a successful livelihood and poverty. The ability to work and maintain a household was the primary measure of success for most people, and ill-health was the swiftest way that life could unravel. Doing everything one could to stay healthy, therefore, was a major preoccupation throughout the period.

Someone living in the eighteenth century would not distinguish, as we do today, the healthiness of their body from their mental, spiritual or moral well-being. All aspects of their person were deeply inter-connected, just as they themselves were connected to the physical and spiritual world around them. In trying to understand changes to their bodies, it was natural to look to changes in the wider universe for explanation, whether that be the seasons of the year, the phases of the moon, or the balance of the humours within and around them.

The widespread understanding of the body's composition was still grounded in the classical theory of the humours, an idea that had survived unchallenged from ancient Greece. A healthy body was one in which the four humours (blood, phlegm, yellow bile and black bile) were balanced in equal parts. This balance was influenced by a person's environment, diet and activities, and imbalances would affect not only physical health but a person's character. Excessive black bile would, for example, lead to a 'melancholic' temperament – despondent and lethargic.

Practical steps to keep the humours balanced included maintaining a balanced diet, seeking a temperate climate, and ensuring sufficient time was devoted to both physical activity and rest. The easiest way to achieve all these was to live in the countryside rather than towns and cities, and country life was accordingly valued as the natural, healthy environment for human habitation. One reason why Chelsea became a 'village of palaces' was because wealthy individuals such as Robert

Opposite: *The Apothecary* by C. Morelot. Although this image depicts a French apothecary, it accurately depicts the work of a respected apothecary throughout western Europe. Apothecaries created medication and so maintained botanical gardens, like that in Chelsea, and small laboratories in their shops to manufacture chemicals such as those depicted here.

Above: Without anesthetic amputation was an excruciating and brutal option that risked death from shock or infection. The screw tourniquet invented in 1712 did, however, reduce the risks of amputation below the knee.

Walpole kept households there for the health of their children. For those who did live in towns, parks and gardens provided a healthy retreat from the ill-humours and noxious gases thought to permeate urban areas.

The research had already begun that would eventually transform this understanding of the human body. By the end of the seventeenth century, dissection was widely, if discreetly, practised by medical students and had led to a far more accurate understanding of human anatomy. The work of Robert Hooke in the late seventeenth century had popularised microscopy and revealed an intricate, detailed world to be examined and understood. Turning the microscope on the human body began to reveal the intricacies of its construction. Throughout the period, discoveries continued to be made and boundaries pushed, such that for those who followed the research these exciting discoveries led to a level of uncertainty and confusion about the state of medical knowledge. It was in this environment that Mary Toft convinced doctors she had given birth to live rabbits and Benjamin Marten's correct theories of the cause of tuberculosis were rejected.

Right: The Mary Toft scandal, Hogarth. In 1726 Mary Toft persuaded various doctors, including the king's surgeon, that she was giving birth to rabbit parts. The resulting scandal increased public distrust of doctors.

Greater understanding of the human body enabled better identification of sickness, but did not as yet offer an alternative explanation or treatment plan to that provided by the classical understanding of the humours. Only in surgery did this new understanding offer new and more effective treatments in the setting of fractures, draining infections and the removal of lesions. So far as the popular understanding and treatment of everyday health issues were concerned, modern discoveries did not displace the theory of the four humours.

A flea from Hooke's *Micrographia*. Before the invention of the microscope, a flea was simply a biting, jumping black dot. No one had imagined that the level of detail which was revealed was even possible at such a small scale, and it seemed to open up a whole new world.

Everyday people's understanding of health also drew on a deep-rooted body of traditional folk wisdom about behaviour that would promote or harm their well-being. Anglican confirmation was a cure for rheumatism; cutting hair at any time other than under a full moon was thought to drain a person's health; while rescuing someone from drowning could result in an aggrieved Death stalking the rescuer to claim their rightful victim. Such received wisdom was not in conflict with the emerging professionalisation of medical care; it was seen as part of the lay medicine practised at home to maintain a healthy family, and co-existed happily with the medical professions for the rest of the century.

Many of the ways that families maintained a healthy home are the same that we practice today to prevent illness, although they took far more effort. Keeping the house, clothes, bedding and bodies of the family clean was a major undertaking. For those who did not produce their own food and lived in towns away from a reliable clean source of water, vetting the food that the family ate was also of the utmost importance. These duties generally fell to mothers and wives and when people did fall ill, they were the first to administer treatments and cures. Indeed, any seventeenth- or eighteenth-century cookbook included treatments and cures for every disease and ailment imaginable. Herbs had been the basis of most medication for centuries and

Right: An early eighteenth-century barber's bowl. Designed to fit around the neck of a man being shaved, it was also used to bleed people when prescribed by a doctor. Only barbers and surgeons would undertake procedures that required cutting the flesh, and together formed a joint guild until 1745.

The Scientists by Rita Greer. (2007) Scientists of all types worked together. Here Robert Hooke is depicted working with Oxford apothecary Dr Cross on an air pump that he designed to investigate the existence and properties of a vacuum.

in the seventeenth century had been more rigorously analysed, most notably by apothecary Nicholas Culpepper in his book *The Complete Herbal* in 1653, which identified many herbal treatments that are the basis for drugs we still use today.

If someone needed a drug which they didn't grow or was too complicated to make, they would go to an apothecary who created drugs from herbs and chemicals prepared in their laboratories, as well as supplying more unusual extracts such as oil of earthworms, supposedly to help a person pass urine. For many people, doctors were too expensive and an apothecary was the only medical expert that they had access to. An apothecary could only offer recommendations on which drugs treated which ailments; they were not allowed to diagnose patients but they did have a monopoly on preparing medications, an activity which doctors and surgeons were not allowed to practise.

Doctors were distinctly higher status than apothecaries and were distinguished by the gold-topped canes they carried and special wigs. They came to people's houses to diagnose illness and advised, or prescribed, courses of treatment and medication. For those who couldn't afford a doctor's call they might consider going to one of the new voluntary hospitals which became available in some towns in the first half of the eighteenth century. However, the treatments could be very severe and most individuals would only go as a last resort, when their traditional cures were exhausted. For the very poor, medical treatment could be received in workhouses, or via the parish nurse who was paid by the parish to tend those who were ill and could not afford treatment. They had very little in common with modern nurses and the care provided was very basic at best, and unhygienic and dangerous at worst.

Despite the time and effort devoted to avoiding illness, people's state of health was precarious. Common ailments that regularly resulted in death were smallpox, influenza, tuberculosis (known as scrufola) and syphilis (known as the great pox). It is estimated that these diseases accounted for almost half of all deaths and could strike anyone at any time regardless of age, gender, wealth or social class.

Above: The Royal College of Physicians, 1725. The Royal College tried to control the medical profession and in the early eighteenth century had a long-running struggle with apothecaries, whom they accused of treating patients instead of keeping to their remit of providing medication.

Left: The town hall in Marseilles during the plague of 1720, by Michel Serre. The plague created scenes of terror as it seemed to create hell on earth. While this proved to be the last outbreak, it continued to haunt the public imagination.

Smallpox was the single biggest killer in Europe during the eighteenth century. A highly contagious disease, with a high mortality rate, it often left its survivors scarred and disfigured. Once contracted, there was no reliable treatment and this, combined with its infection rate, made people very scared of the outbreaks which periodically swept across the country. Smallpox could only be contracted once, however, and this led to the development of an early form of inoculation, brought to England by Lady Mary Wortley Montagu in 1721. This involved purposely giving people a small dose of smallpox in the hope they would suffer only mild symptoms, and thereafter be protected. But it was not without risk and 10 per cent of those inoculated developed full-blown smallpox. This led some doctors to distrust the foreign treatment, brought into the country by a woman, but Lady Mary's place in society meant that the aristocracy, including the royal family, embraced inoculation, guaranteeing it a level of credibility.

The high fevers caused by influenzas could be very dangerous. The flu hadn't been identified as a specific disease, although the term was first coined in 1703 and named as the cause of the pandemic in 1743, and we can now also identify other outbreaks in the seventeenth and eighteenth centuries as influenza. High temperatures were thought to be caused by too much blood and so bleeding was a common treatment. Bleeding was a popular but counterproductive treatment for most illnesses in the eighteenth century but in the case of influenza it actually saved lives. As influenza commonly causes death by filling the lungs with liquid, removing large quantities of blood lowered blood pressure to such a level that the lungs emptied, averting a fatal crisis.

Tuberculosis was not identified as one disease either and there was no reliable treatment; but tuberculosis of the lymph nodes had been designated as scrufola and for centuries had been treated by the royal touch. This was a belief common to the English and French crowns that the monarch's touch could cure the disease. Queen Anne was the last British monarch to carry out this ceremonial and religious duty, but it is debatable whether many of those who were touched actually believed they were likely to be cured, or rather just wanted the opportunity to see the queen.

While smallpox, influenza and tuberculosis accounted for approximately half of deaths in Britain in the first half of the eighteenth century, it was the plague that was the most feared disease not only in Britain, but throughout the whole of Europe. The bubonic plague had periodically and terribly swept across the continent since the

The Chelsea water works. The eighteenth century saw the growth of water companies like this that delivered piped river water into the centre of towns and cities, to the great benefit of the health of the inhabitants. However the water was generally unfiltered and still not safe to drink.

thirteenth century, with devastating results. It haunted people's imaginations as an apocalyptic spectre. The last outbreak in Britain was that of 1665 and its horrors remained fresh in people's memories. When it broke out in Marseilles in 1720, swiftly killing 100,000 people, the rest of Europe held its breath in fear. In England, Defoe wrote a vivid fictionalised account of the horrors of the 1665 plague as a dramatic public health warning to the nation and to reconcile the nation to the unpopular Quarantine Act of 1721/22.

Life was precarious and suffering and death could strike at any moment. The sudden death of Queen Anne's son William in 1700, and the incredible sufferings of Queen Caroline's deathbed in 1737 were stark reminders that youth, wealth and privilege offered no protection. When death came it was marked as a momentous and highly formal event. The ceremonies and rituals surrounding death were an attempt to imprint on people's minds a vivid impression of the departed that would last for the rest of their lives. The body was dressed in the deceased's finest clothes, with the face painted by an undertaker. The body then lay in state for several days, during which friends, family and even casual acquaintances would visit. The belief in salvation and an afterlife after death was essentially universal, and even those who had only set foot in church to marry would return in death. In the funeral service the minister would give an oration on the good example set by the departed, whether in their personal relationships, religious practices or good works, and urge the congregation to take heed. Afterwards a funeral procession accompanied the coffin, consisting only of men who were generally robed in white if the deceased was young and unmarried or otherwise robed in black.

PLACES TO VISIT

56, 58 Artillery Lane, Bethnal Green, London E1 7LS.
Two examples of high-quality purpose-built mid-eighteenth-century shops.

Assembly Rooms, Blake Street, York YO1 2QG.
First used in 1732 these rooms are a beautiful example of the new type of commercial/public sociability that developed in the first half of the eighteenth century.

St Bartholomew's Museum, St Bartholomew's Hospital, West Smithfield, London EC1A 7BE. Tel. 0203 4655798.
The hospital was redesigned by John Gibbs in 1728 into a formal classical square. The museum traces the history of medicine from the hospital's foundation in the thirteenth century and provides a good overview of eighteenth-century medicine.

Bevis Marks Synagogue, 2 Henage Lane, London EC3A 5DQ.
Completed in 1701 in response to the growth of London's Jewish community, this is Britain's oldest synagogue and was the religious centre of the Anglo-Jewish world throughout the eighteenth century.

The Black Country Living Museum, Tipton Road, Dudley DY1 4SQ. Tel. 01215 579643.
Contains the only working model of Thomas Newcomen's steam engine.

Chelsea Physic Garden, 66 Royal Hospital Road, London SW3 4HS. Tel. 0207 3496458.
Opened in 1673, in 1713 it was leased in perpetuity to the apothecaries by the king's physician, Sir Hans Sloane, and became the world's most important botanical garden.

Christ Church, Fournier Street, Spitalfields, London E1 6QE. Tel. 0207 8593035.
A beautiful example of an early eighteenth-century parish church, designed by Nicholas Hawksmoor, 1714–29.

Coalbrookdale Museum of Iron, Coach Road, Coalbrookdale, Telford TF8 7DQ. Tel. 01952 433424.
Exhibition around the remains of Abraham Darby's factory where he perfected the smelting of iron with coke instead of charcoal, one of the essential advances for the industrial revolution.

Derby's Museum of Industry and History, Silk Mill Lane, Derby DE1 3AF. Tel. 01332 642234.
This museum is on the site of Britain's earliest mill dating from 1717–21.

Erddig Hall, Wrexham, Wales LL13 0YT. Tel. 01978 355314.
Although Erddig is not a typical house it features particularly complete eighteenth-century interiors and gardens.

The Geffrye Museum, Kingsland Road, Shoreditch E2 8EA. Tel. 0207 7399893.

Museum dedicated to depicting the changing style of the English domestic interior in a series of period rooms from 1600 to the present day.

The George Inn, 77 Borough High Street, Southwark, London SE1 1NH. Tel. 0207 4072056.

This late seventeenth-century inn is the last surviving galleried inn that would have been typical throughout the eighteenth century.

Hogarth House and *Chiswick House*, Chiswick, London W4 2QN.

William Hogarth's summer retreat, built *c*. 1700, is a good example of a comfortable house belonging to one of the well-off 'middling sort.' Almost adjacent, Chiswick House demonstrates the Palladian principles that came to dominate architecture in the eighteenth century.

Lawrence Street, Chelsea, London.

In this small street you can see the first home of the Chelsea Porcelain Factory and several fine examples of early eighteenth-century houses.

Llanon Cottage in Ceredigion Museum, Terrace Road, Aberystwyth, Dyfed, Wales SY23 2AQ. Tel. 01970 633088.

A beautifully preserved rural cottage typical of the early eighteenth century.

The National Maritime Museum, Romney Road, Greenwich SE10 9NF and *The Royal Observatory*, Blackheath Avenue SE10 8XJ. Tel. 0208 8584422.

The museum buildings were constructed in the early eighteenth century as a hospital for retired seamen. The observatory was a focus for scientific research as the only purpose-built scientific building of the period.

Salvat's Coffee House, St Margaret's Street, Bradford-on-Avon, Wiltshire BA15 1DE. Tel. 01225 867474.

An original early eighteenth-century coffee house.

Spitalfields, London.

This district is dominated by late seventeenth-/early eighteenth-century streets of terraced houses built for prosperous silk workers and artisans.

Stowe Landscape Gardens, Buckingham, Buckinghamshire MK18 5DQ. Tel. 01280 822850.

The magnificent gardens at Stowe demonstrate the shift from formal landscape design to a more 'natural' appearance.

Victoria and Albert Museum, Cromwell Road, South Kensington, London SW7 2RL. Tel. 020 7942 2000.

Includes beautiful examples of eighteenth-century clothes and porcelain, and exhibitions on tea drinking and Vauxhall Gardens.

Weald and Downland Open Air Museum, Chichester, Sussex PO18 0EU. Tel. 01243 811348.

Large site containing over fifty excellent examples of vernacular English buildings. Of particular interest are the early eighteenth-century cattle sheds, brick-drying shed, court barn, granary, stable and watermill.

INDEX

Page numbers in italic refer to illustrations

Agriculture 12, 32, 33–4, *33*, 35, 43
Alcohol *30*, 35–6, *42*, 57–8
Anne, Queen *6*, 76, 77
Apothecaries 70, 74, *74*, *75*
Apprenticeships 15, 20, 31–2, *32*, *41*, 47, 67, 69
Artisans/craftsmen 8, 37, *37*
Banks/banknotes *8*, 10
Beauty, features of *49*
Books/book-reading 45, 63, *69*
Children *14*, 15, 19, *64*, 65: education of *64*, 65–9, 66, *69*; and work 12, 31–2, *32*, *33*, 37, 67, 68, 69
Church/churches *10*, 16, *22*, 23
Clothing: children's *49*, *49*, 65; clergical *10*; men's *14*, 16, *46*, 47, 48, 49; women's *14*, 16–17, *24*, *44*, *46*, 47, *47*, 48–9, *48*, *49*
Coal mining *11*, 55, *55*
Community/national celebrations 23–4, *24*, 58–9
Contraception 19
Crime and punishment 27–9, *27*, *28*, *29*
Darby, Abraham 40
Death 26, 75, 76, 77
Defoe, Daniel 10, 63, 67, 77
Disposable income *8*, *8*
Doctors 15, 55, 72, 74–5
Domestic service/servants 20, 26, 32–3, 35–6
Drugs, making of 73–4, *74*
Economic

boom/revolution 7–9, 36–7, 45, *50*, 55, *55*
Education, role of parents *64*, 65–6, 66, 67, *67*
Enclosure (of land) 12, 33
Factories/workshops 12, 31, 35–7, 40
Fairs/festivities *13*, 23–4, *25*, 59
Families 20: composition of 15; parish support of 27; and work *33*, 36–7
Family life *14*, *19*, *56*, 57, 65
Fiennes, Celia 52–3
Folk wisdom 73
Food: preparation of 5, 20, *38*, 39–41, *41*, *42*, *42*, 43; prices 43; supply/variety of 33–4, 45
Gambling *17*, 61–2, *61*
Gonson, John *29*
Herbs, use as medicine 73–4
Highwaymen 53, *55*
Hogarth, William *17*, *19*, *26*, 27, *29*, *32*, *41*, *56*, *72*
Hospitals *35*, 37, 75
Houses/households *14*–21, *19*: and family life 15–16; design features/use of rooms *14*, *18*, 20–1, *21*, *38*, 39–40: kitchens/parlours *18*, *20*, 21, *21*, 31, 39–40, *40*, *41*; and health 73; 'keeping' of *19*, 45–6; setting up of *18*; personal space *19*, 20–1; working in *33*, 36
Illness and disease 73, 77: influenza 13, 75, 76; plague *75*, 76–7; smallpox 13, 75, 76; syphilis 75;

tuberculosis 72, 75, 76; typhus 13
Industrialisation 8, *11*, 12, *30*, *33*, 35–6
Ireland 13
Jacobite uprisings 9–10, 24
Journeymen 31, 36, 47
Landowners 9, 11, 24, 52
Life, attitude to 8
Literacy rates 69
Marriage/weddings 15–19, *16*, *17*, *18*
Mary Wortley Montagu, Lady 76
Meals/mealtimes *14*, 41–3, *43*, 57
Medical knowledge/medicine 70, 72–3, *72*, *73*, 76
'Middling sort' 8, 12, *14*, *20*, 21, 35, *58*, 68
Moral virtues 66, 67
Mortality rates 19
National debt 7, 10–11
Parish life 24–9, *22*, *25*, 51
Parliament *4*, 6, 7, 9, 12, 63
Politics 8–10, *10*, 11–12, 62–3
Poor (the) 26: accommodation 20–1; medical treatment 75; parish relief 25–7; work 31
Population growth 12–13, 69
Print media/printing 36, 54, 57, *62*, 63, 69
Prisoners/prisons 27
Prostitution *27*, *28*, *29*
Public health 77
Religious belief *10*, 16, 23, 69
Road network/travel 24, 51–4, *51*, *52*, *53*
Royal family *6*, 7, 9,

23, 24, 52, 58
Schools/schooling 66, 66, 68–9: types of 68–9, *69*
Scotland *6*, 7, 12, 13, 23, 54, 69
Shops/shopkeepers 8, *10*, *44*, 45, *46*, 47
South Sea Bubble crisis 5, 10–12
Spinsters 33, *35*, 37
Sport 59–61, *60*, 62
Taxation/taxes 12, 24
Tea making/taking *20*, 21, *42*, 55
Teaching aids/tools 67, *68*, *69*
'The Great Frost' 13, *13*
Theatre and plays 62–3
Toft, Mary 72, *72*
Toll/turnpike roads 51–2, *52*, *53*
Trade cards 36, *46*, 55
Trades/tradesmen 8, 15, 31–2, *34*, 36–7, *36*, *37*, 47
Transport and travel (modes of) 52–5, *52*, *53*, *54*, 55; use of roads 24, 51–4, *51*, *52*, *53*
Turnpike trusts 51–2, *52*
Wages 12, 36
Wales 7, 12, 13, 54, 69
Walpole, Sir Robert 5, 12, 62–3, 71–2
Wealth, generation of 8, 9, *9*, 10–11, 31
Wesley, John 10
Women: status of 15, 26; and duties/work 12, *20*, 26, 27, 31, 32, 33, 34–5, *33*, 36, *38*, *42*, 59, *64*, *65*, 66, 67, 73; and marriage 15–16, *16*, *18*; status of 15, 26
Work/work practices 12, 25, 31, 36–7, 37
Workhouses 25, 27, 75